T0318829

The Perils of Populism

The Feminist Bookshelf: Ideas for the 21st Century
A Project of the Institute for Research on Women at
Rutgers University

The Perils of Populism

EDITED BY SARAH TOBIAS AND
ARLENE STEIN

Rutgers University Press

New Brunswick, Camden, and Newark, New Jersey, and London

Names: Tobias, Sarah, 1963– editor. | Stein, Arlene, editor.
Title: The perils of populism / edited by Sarah Tobias and Arlene Stein.
Description: New Brunswick, NJ : Rutgers University Press, [2022] |
Series: The feminist bookshelf: Ideas for the 21st century |
Includes bibliographical references and index.
Identifiers: LCCN 2021055668 | ISBN 9781978825307 (paperback) |
ISBN 9781978825314 (hardback) | ISBN 9781978825321 (epub) |
ISBN 9781978825338 (mobi) | ISBN 9781978825345 (pdf)
Subjects: LCSH: Populism. | Right and left (Political science) |
Authoritarianism. | Violence. | Feminist theory. | Marginality, Social
Classification: LCC JC423 .P36354 2022 | DDC 320.56/62—dc23/eng/20220327
LC record available at https://lccn.loc.gov/2021055668

A British Cataloging-in-Publication record for this book is available
from the British Library.

♾ The paper used in this publication meets the requirements of the American
National Standard for Information Sciences—Permanence of Paper for
Printed Library Materials, ANSI Z39.48-1992.

www.rutgersuniversitypress.org

Manufactured in the United States of America

To all those who pursue justice and seek to heal the world

Contents

Introduction   1

SARAH TOBIAS AND ARLENE STEIN

1. Fragile Democracies in a Post-Truth Era   26

   KHADIJAH COSTLEY WHITE, CYNTHIA MILLER-IDRISS,
   AND VALENTINE M. MOGHADAM

2. Dispossession: Gender and the Construction
   of Us / Them Dichotomies   55

   SABINE HARK

3. Ascetic Masculinity and Right-Wing Populism
   in Hindu Nationalist India   72

   AMRITA BASU

4. Hegemony as Capitalist Strategy:
   For a Neo-Marxian Critique of Financialized
   Capitalism   109

   NANCY FRASER

5. Feminism and the Anti-Trump Resistance   131

   L. A. KAUFFMAN

6. Organizing for Power: The Grassroots Struggle
   for Inclusive Democracy   149

   HEATHER BOOTH, JYL JOSEPHSON,
   AND SCOT NAKAGAWA

Acknowledgments 173

Notes on Contributors 175

Index 185

The Perils of Populism

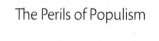

Introduction

SARAH TOBIAS AND ARLENE STEIN

Populism is an approach to politics that pits "the people" against "the elite." Whether understood as an ideology (Mudde and Kaltwasser 2017), a strategy (Weyland 2018; Laclau 2005; Mouffe 2005, 2018), or a set of performances (Moffitt 2016), populism is a rebuke to established ways of doing politics and often to established political parties too. It is neither inherently left nor right in its orientation. Though there have been left-wing movements of a populist bent, in recent years a right-wing populism that combines nationalism and xenophobia has been ascendant. In Britain, for example, a majority of voters embraced Brexit, which champions the nation-state against regional and global cooperation. In Brazil, Far-Right candidate Jair Bolsonaro won a landslide victory in the 2018 presidential election, after campaigning with the slogan "Brazil above everything, God above everyone" (quoted in Fishman 2018). And in the United States, businessman Donald Trump swept into the highest public office by promising to challenge elite corruption and restore white Christian supremacy.

It is not as though democratic systems had been working effectively. Over the past several decades, political and economic elites have weakened the social welfare functions of states, substituting in their place a market-based neoliberalism. Neoliberalism seeks to reconfigure the polity in all its dimensions: economic, political, social, and cultural. Neoliberal states act in ways that are centaur-like, "uplifting and 'liberating'" those who already hold cultural and economic capital, but increasingly "castigatory and restrictive" toward those who suffer from economic insecurity, according to sociologist Loïc Wacquant (2012, 74). In such environments, characterized by a go-it-alone ethos on the one hand, and increasing inequality on the other, right-wing populism has gained a foothold.

Populism, according to political theorist Cas Mudde, is an "illiberal democratic response" to growing "undemocratic liberalism" (2021). Rather than encouraging democratic debate, a better representative system, and economic redistribution, it often emboldens authoritarian leaders who have much more in common with the corrupt elite than with "the people" writ large. Even so, these leaders frequently claim to represent "the people"—by which they mean those segments of the population that authoritarian leaders selectively rate as good or worthy, true patriots, or bearers of "common sense." The power of authoritarian leaders depends on their capacity to divide the polity. They tend to be more than willing to trample on minority rights. As Brazil's Bolsonaro so succinctly puts it, "The law must exist to defend the majorities. Minorities must fit in or simply disappear!" (quoted in Fishman 2018). Demonizing minority communities helps these leaders fuel social polarization, racism, and violence, and spread the belief that society is facing crises that these leaders (and they alone) can fix.

Once in office, populist leaders consolidate power by sowing popular distrust of scientists, journalists, and others that complex societies depend on in order to function effectively. Witness former U.S. president Donald Trump's repeated efforts to discredit the media and popularize the term "fake news." This is a contemporary form of post-truth politics. "Post-truth" was *Oxford Dictionaries* 2016 "international word of the year," defined as "relating to or denoting circumstances in which objective facts are less influential in shaping public opinion than appeals to emotion and personal belief" (Oxford Languages 2016). The impact of post-truth politics is heightened on social media, as populists flood platforms like Facebook and Twitter with misinformation dissembling as facts. Social media, with its ability to communicate through sound bites and at lightning speed, has also proved a reliable way for populist leaders and their supporters to provoke violence against demonized minorities, immigrants, and stigmatized others. So, while there may be some very good reasons for the emergence of popular discontent, populist movements, especially on the Right, can be exceedingly dangerous.

One may ask what this has to do with gender and feminism. A great deal, it turns out. Gender shapes how the powerful mobilize, how social issues are framed, and whose narratives—and lives—count. Gender intersects with race, sexuality, nationality, and class in generating support for, as well as resistance toward, social and political movements. Rage against the political system is frequently articulated in gendered terms as a defense of hegemonic masculinity, reinforcing gender binaries and hierarchies and punishing those who transgress them. Feminist scholars and activists and others who challenge gender-based discrimination and promote social justice find themselves at odds with the repressive priorities of right-wing populists. Consequently, they have been at the helm of many recent efforts to contest authoritarian populism and reinvigorate democracy, as seen in the global groundswell catalyzed by the 2017 Women's March.

Gender and Right-Wing Populism

Gender has been a central aspect of right-wing populism, though it is not always explicitly stated. Many right-wing populist movements call for women's return to "traditional" roles as wives, homemakers, and mothers. They see women as producers of the nation whose role is conceived largely in terms of maintaining traditional households, raising children, and supporting their breadwinner husbands. Historically, within right-wing populist movements, women play key roles supporting these notions of gender hierarchy, such as among the extreme right (Blee 2008). A related literature considers the role of men in defending versions of hegemonic masculinity that position them as protectors of the family (Kimmel 2017).

Calling for the preservation of gender hierarchies, contemporary right-wing populist movements around the world embrace the heteronormative nuclear family and attack reproductive rights, sex education, and LGBTQ rights. Animating such politics is a belief in essentialized understandings of sex, which conflate sex and gender. In the United States, since the 1970s, many formations of right-wing populisms include religious fundamentalisms based in evangelical Protestantism and conservative Catholicism, which have waged varied "culture wars" against abortion, sex education, and LGBTQ rights (Hunter 1992; Stein 2001). They cast gay people, supporters of women's abortion rights, and proponents of sexual education as immoral individuals who challenge the "natural" dichotomy of the sexes and the authority of fathers. They charge that an underserving elite class exerts an outsized influence on and manipulates the state and its institutions in order to carry out their liberal agenda. And they use affect and the emotions, such as anger, shame, and rage, to amplify their message and to gain adherents.

The new millennium has seen the rise of a global right-ward turn (Graff, Kapur, Walters 2019) for whom gender politics is central. It is animated by a defense against "gender ideology." This movement began in Europe and Latin America, as conservative Catholic activists sought to discredit gender studies programs and scholars of gender, whom they accused of being ideological, pseudoreligious, and propagating pseudoscience (Corredor 2019). Antigenderism unites various strands of the Right and offers a powerful new language for nationalist sentiment (Graff 2014). Antigender advocates argue that feminist and queer notions of gender threaten a presumed natural social order, promote homosexuality, and induce gender confusion. They use secular and faith-based arguments to assert that efforts to question the essential nature of gender and sexuality are unscientific, indeed dangerous.

The attack on so-called gender ideology informs campaigns that focus on transgender children, particularly in the United States, raising questions about whether individuals are capable of clearly articulating their desires and choices for medical technologies, such as puberty blockers and cross-gender hormones (Meadow 2018). These right-wing campaigns also targeted individuals' right to claim new gender identities without undergoing body modifications, and to occupy public spaces on that basis.

Writing of common features of right-wing populisms in the contemporary European context, Dietze and Roth (2020) note that "populism is not only concerned with gender as an issue itself but also with gender as a meta-language for negotiating different conditions of inequality and power in the context of current struggles over hegemony, and over resources forged by neoliberalism" (8). Observers note that neoliberalism exacerbates the inequalities that feed white working and middle-class anxieties, making populist appeals attractive. Indeed, struggles against the very notion of gender became a "symbolic glue" for a spectrum of reactionary forces—authoritarian and ethnonationalist (Kováts and Põim, 2015).

White nationalists in the United States and Europe are obsessed with fears of "white genocide," the imagined biological extinction of the white race, which they attribute to immigration growth among Black and Brown people, as well as to gender and sexual liberalism, which they believe is depressing white birthrates. They claim that Jews, especially Jewish elites in education and government, play a pivotal role in orchestrating this existential threat. The growing influence of the "alt-right," propelled in large part by social media, has meant that racist ideas such as these, which "previously lurked in the shadows of the unspeakable," writes historian Alexandra Minna Stern, "have migrated into everyday discourse, becoming imaginable and utterable" (2019, 8). Leaders such as Donald Trump offered an additional impetus, making voicing such ideas more permissible.

This set the stage for battles against "critical race theory," a body of literature which argued that white supremacy of the past lives on in the laws and societal rules of the present. "Elites are enforcing a set of manners and cultural limits, they're seeking to reengineer the foundation of human psychology and social institutions through the new politics of race," proclaimed one spokesman (Wallace-Wells 2021). Again, as in all populist campaigns, elites are the problem. For conservatives, critical race theory and gender theories represent elite worldviews that are anathema to the status quo and threaten white Christian supremacy.

Both gender identity and critical race theory teach that hierarchies of race and gender are not natural. They are humanmade social arrangements, which are therefore malleable. Much as it once targeted Marxism and the movements inspired by it, now right-wing populists battle critical race and gender thought, stoking fears of a great nefarious conspiracy to take over the culture. The figure of the innocent, vulnerable child who is the unwitting victim of liberal indoctrination, has come to symbolize national purity, and at times racial purity (Gill Peterson 2021; Stern 2019). These are battles about the nature of social differences, whose lives deserve to be protected, and who should make decisions about those lives and allocate resources to protect them. They are struggles over cultural power.

Populism, Gender, and Political Power

Of course, populism is a struggle for political power too. Some scholars differentiate between populism as a social movement that pressures government to change policy and practice, and populism as a movement aspiring to exercise power in the name of the people. Thus Hirschmann suggests the importance of differentiating between "popular protest movements," which are attempts "to get government to change its ways—to change its laws, to change its interpretation of those laws, to change its practices," and "populist movements," which constitute efforts to "exercise power . . . extra-governmentally" (2021). The Trump supporters who marched down Pennsylvania Avenue in the aftermath of the 2020 election to riot at the U.S. Capitol are in the latter category. This group was predominantly white and male and sought to "to threaten, intimidate, and silence" all those who got in its way. Their violent actions were both racialized and gendered assertions of political power: "the expression of a distorted version of white masculinity that resents the perceived loss of position if racial and sexual equality are established" (Hirschmann 2021). They were galvanized to act through an understanding of popular sovereignty, "the notion that the people are the fundamental source of authority in modern politics" (Grattan 2014, 180).

This notion of popular sovereignty is intrinsic to both democracy and populism. It has prompted some scholars, such as Laclau and Mouffe, to equate left-wing populism with the concept of radical democracy. These scholars consider left-wing populism to be "democracy at its best, because the will of the people is constructed through the people's direct mobilization and consent. It is also politics at its best, because it employs only discursive devices and the art of persuasion" (Urbinati 2019, 117). Some advocates of left-wing populism argue that its success is measured by its capacity to nurture respect for pluralism and egalitarianism, a mindset fostered by the practice of grassroots politics (Grattan 2014, 182). Left-wing populists have sought to "mobilize across race, class, gender, sexuality, and nationality" to pursue justice—including for women and LGBTQ people—on a global scale (Roth 2018). Yet, although left-wing populism encourages inclusion and "experiments with horizontality" (Grattan 2014, 197), it may still exclude groups situated at society's margins. Grattan observes that progressive Bernie Sanders initially ignored issues of racial justice in his 2016 campaign for democratic presidential nominee. It took repeated confrontations with Black Lives Matter activists for him to question his campaign's "material and affective attachments to whiteness" (2020, 137). Similarly, McKean (2016) cautions that it is too easy for left-wing populists to treat "the people" as homogeneous rather than equal; a tendency toward homogeneity reinforces the "othering" of those who are perennially and structurally marginalized.

While left-wing populists advocate for a broad and inclusive conception of "the people," right-wing populist understandings of "the people" are usually partial rather than pluralistic, saturated with moral rectitude, and pitted against external others (even if these "others" also inhabit the polity). Populism and nationalism often collide at this juncture. As Mostov notes, "The polarization of 'us' and 'them' in populism draws on nationalist notions of exclusive belonging, the need for closure to protect the 'us' from would be infiltrators, and observance of proscribed gendered roles to ensure the continued rule of the majority (race/ethno-nation)" (2021). Right-wing populist movements see themselves as defenders of "ordinary men and women" against elites and members of minoritized groups, who champion ideas that are considered anathema to the majority. The preservation of gender and racial hierarchies, and the drawing of distinctions between "natives" and "others" are key aspects of such movements. Farris (2017) asserts that feminist scholarship is pivotal for explaining how nationalists instrumentalize women's rights discourse for their own political advantage, such as by depicting Muslim women as victims who need to be "saved" from oppression while demonizing Muslim and non-Western immigrant men.

Crucially, right-wing populism is not only an oppositional force; it is a movement that aspires toward government. Populists typically win elections when a charismatic individual leads his party to victory. This leader "valorize[s] the relationship between masculinity and politics" by performing as a "potentially violent 'strongman'" who perpetuates a cult of leadership with a focus on "action," "anti-intellectualism," "and the leader's virility" (Löffler, Luyt, and Starck 2020, 1, 3). He invariably portrays himself "as the personification of the people" (de la Torre 2017, 40). When women such as Marine Le Pen in France lead right-wing populist parties, they tap into and perform aspects of this "political masculinity" alongside "political femininity" (Geva 2020). What the primacy of leadership implies, as Urbinati astutely observes, is that when populists attain power they perform a type of "direct representation" that posits an unmediated "relationship between the leader and the people" (2019, 124). Yet, since populist leaders represent only a segment of the people rather than the whole, and claim that this segment is both "the measure of political justice and legitimacy" *and* embodied in their person, what emerges is a type of "extreme majoritarianism," where the leader vows to "emancipate" his followers by "avenging them against the other part or parts of the populace" (Urbinati 2019, 113, 120). The implications of populism as "direct representation" are therefore profoundly dangerous for those minoritized groups expunged from "the people."

There is a strange, if crude, resemblance between the relationship that right-wing populist leaders construct with their followers and the relationship between sovereign and subjects in Thomas Hobbes's *Leviathan* (1651). In *Leviathan*, men (and the emphasis is on *men*) make a social contract among each other to replace self-government with the sovereign's government, authorize his acts as their own, and agree that he "beare their Person" ([1651] 1968, 227, 228). The subjects-to-be confer "all their power and strength upon one Man, or upon one Assembly of Men, that may reduce all their Wills, by plurality of voices, unto one will" ([1651] 1968, 227). The sovereign, who is not party to this contract, acquires absolute power to prevent disorder. Pateman describes social contract theory as "the greatest story of masculine political birth"—as men alone are party to the hypothetical contract; women remain subjugated to their husbands and ineligible to be part of this foundational agreement (1989, 451); "If the representer is to be unified, he must be *he*" (Pateman 1989, 461). Similarly, Mills, who describes the social contract as both a hypothetical and a nonideal phenomenon, emphasizes that the social contract "is . . . between just the people who count, the people who really are people ("we the white people"). So it is a Racial Contract" (1997, 3). It may be that Hobbesian contractarianism and contemporary right-wing populism are more similar than different in terms of who is incorporated into the people (a part, masquerading as a whole), endowed with political agency, or elevated to leadership roles. Under these circumstances, it should certainly come as no surprise that contemporary right-wing populists perform "political masculinity" or that their politics often takes an authoritarian turn, attacking freedom of speech, the press, and assembly—those features of a robust public sphere that enable social justice movements to articulate their demands for liberation.

The chapters in this volume explore the relationship between gender, populism, and democracy through a feminist lens. They capture some of the most dynamic, interdisciplinary work presented at the Institute for Research on Women (IRW) at Rutgers University as we collectively tried to make sense of the Trump era and its relationship to global threats to democracy.[1] Four of the authors whose essays are featured in this book—Amrita Basu, Nancy Fraser, Sabine Hark, and L. A. Kauffman—participated in IRW's Distinguished Lecture Series on "The Perils of Populism: Feminist Conversations" during 2017–2018. Two years later, our programming centered on the related theme, "This Is What Democracy Looks Like: Feminist Reimaginings." As part of this series, we organized a roundtable, "Just the Facts: Fragile Democracies in a Post-Truth Era," which addressed concerns related to populism and authoritarianism. Cynthia Miller-Idriss, Valentine M. Moghadam, and Khadijah White co-created a piece that reflects that discussion. The edited transcript of a second panel on "Organizing for Power: The Grassroots Struggle for Inclusive Democracy," featuring activists and thinkers Heather Booth, Scot Nakagawa, and Jyl Josephson, appears here as well.

Together, the essays in this volume explore the growth of populism, authoritarianism, and nationalism in the United States, the Middle East, Europe, and India. They offer distinctively feminist perspectives on the threat to democratic stability and contribute to a rapidly expanding literature on gender and the Far Right. In chapter 1, "Fragile Democracies in a Post-Truth Era," scholars Valentine Moghadam, Cynthia Miller-Idriss, and Khadijah White show that populism is a global phenomenon, occurring in the aftermath of the Arab Spring in the Middle East as well as in regions as diverse as Latin America, Europe, and the United States. While populist leaders claim that their rule will protect the nation from internal and external threats, authoritarians disdain the truth, and deploy widespread disinformation. As scientific expertise and facts are denigrated, democracies become fragile and easily manipulated. For feminists to effectively challenge right-wing populism and reinvigorate democracy, Miller-Idriss argues that they would need, among other things, to resist the ongoing dismissal of scientific expertise and propagation of "alternative facts." They should also challenge dominant metrics of success and notions of the good society. In a different perspective, Moghadam calls for a transnational "*social feminism* that supports economic justice and wealth redistribution and stands in solidarity with striking teachers, factory workers, and minority groups." This would oppose militarism and violence against women, and forge alliances with youth advocating for climate justice. Finally, White, calls for "a Black feminist lens that centers oppression and inequality," and moves beyond a "post-truth society" by challenging the epistemological premises that have enabled elites to retain power through discriminatory and exclusionary means.

Divisive rhetoric around race, ethnicity, and gender often plays a key role in mobilizing right-wing populism. German feminist Sabine Hark's chapter, "Dispossession: Gender and the Construction of Us / Them Dichotomies" (chapter 2) adroitly illustrates the interplay between polemics and politics. Hark describes the "unifying ideological platform" that binds right-wing populists and nationalists in Germany, which manifests as vicious attacks against the field of gender studies and the concept of "gender ideology." The resulting discourse of "anti-genderism" rejects LGBTIQ rights and sex education, and espouses racist Islamophobia. It repeatedly invokes an us / them dichotomy, with the "people" on one side, and gender studies professors or the gender lobby in Brussels on the other. What "gender ideology" means in this context is amorphous, yet its authoritarian critics often depict it as a conspiracy or "a totalitarian project" akin to "communism or fascism," which "threatens the natural and divine order of the sexes, heterosexual marriage, the family, and indeed the very foundation of Western society." According to Hark, antigenderism is "not only an element of an authoritarian, neoreactionary worldview that aims to undermine democracy as such," it is also a right-wing tool that serves to reinforce numerous "policies of exclusion."

In chapter 3, "Ascetic Masculinity and Right-Wing Populism in Hindu Nationalist India," political scientist Amrita Basu explores how the Bharatiya Janata Party, which has held power in India since 2014, deploys Hindu nationalism as a populist strategy. Although India has been a democracy since 1947, and nominally secular since 1976, it retains constitutional provisions that privilege its Hindu majority. Indian prime minister Narendra Modi has exploited these provisions to exacerbate Hindu nationalism and target women, Muslims, Christians, and other opponents of his regime, often advocating for (or supporting) violence against minorities.

Despite Modi's failure to execute economic reforms and his assault on democratic freedoms, the Indian prime minister remains remarkably popular. Basu argues that Modi's appropriation of Gandhi's performance of sexual renunciation is key to understanding this appeal.

In chapter 4, socialist feminist theorist Nancy Fraser argues in "Hegemony as Capitalist Strategy" that state-managed capitalism, which was the hallmark of the mid-twentieth century, has been superseded by a globalized capitalism where banks, rather than democratic institutions, set the rules of engagement. This has resulted in a crisis for contemporary democracies. The existence of transnational corporations and other powerful, private entities means that governments are no longer able to effectively implement policies on many major issues. Meanwhile, the public is becoming increasingly resistant to politics-as-usual, leading to the growth of reactionary and progressive populism. Reactionary populism is "antiglobalist," combining "strict immigration controls for 'outsiders' . . . [with] generous social provision for 'insiders.'" By contrast, progressive populism combines an expansive understanding of community, including "opposition to gender, racist, and anti-immigrant violence," with a redistributive economic ethos that focuses on "job creation and financial reform." Only progressive populism has the potential to defeat neoliberalism's economic and political hegemony. However, progressive populists confront substantial opposition from both reactionary populists and progressive neoliberals, who now have the upper hand.

In chapter 5, "Feminism and the Anti-Trump Resistance," activist L. A. Kauffman, who helped organize a number of nationwide protests against the rise of authoritarianism in the United States, explores the huge groundswell of opposition to President Trump that developed in the aftermath of the

November 2016 election. She asks why this opposition is so rarely characterized as feminist, despite feminism's centrality to early resistance efforts. The 2017 Women's March, for instance, was the largest ever same-day mass mobilization in U.S. history. Its leadership was driven by feminist values, which were expressed through the march's intersectional Unity Principles. While acknowledging that misogyny clearly played a role in marginalizing the feminist resistance story, Kauffman notes that "organizing weaknesses" were central to the sidelining of feminism. She describes the difficulties of creating a national organization—Women's March Inc.—out of the myriad grassroots Women's March campaigns. Despite their success in centering racial justice and the leadership of women of color, Women's March Inc. faced many challenges, due both to the exceptional circumstances in which it was created and the difficulties of creating a feminist-focused, organizing-oriented nonprofit in a neoliberal era. Progressive populists confront internal difficulties as they challenge their counterparts on both the Right and the neoliberal Left, as Kauffman shows.

We end with a roundtable discussion in chapter 6, "Organizing for Power: The Grassroots Struggle for Inclusive Democracy," which features leading organizers and strategists Heather Booth, Scot Nakagawa, and Jyl Josephson. In the contemporary United States, atomized communities, unaccountable corporate power, and the pervasive growth of authoritarianism and white nationalism threaten democracy. The authors express concern about the ways atrophied social bonds and political disengagement foster the rise of authoritarianism. Community organizing, they argue, is a potential antidote—and a mechanism for strengthening American democracy. Collectively, they describe some of the most successful organizing strategies to promote progressive, political change.

The economy plays a central role in the populist resurgence. For Nancy Fraser, the economy is not just a backdrop to the development of populism, but a central factor contributing to its appeal. In chapter 4, she describes the political contradiction at capitalism's core: legitimate and effective government is a prerequisite for "sustained capital accumulation," but it can also be undermined by the flow of capital. This is particularly the case when "capital's drive toward boundless accumulation becomes unmoored from political control and turns against its own conditions of possibility." In such conditions, the "economy overruns polity, eating away at public power and destabilizing the very political agencies on which capital depends." Such aggressive capitalism results in two types of political crisis: institutional and hegemonic. In the former, governments are "outgunned by private powers" and consequently "lack the necessary heft to govern effectively." The second type of crisis occurs when "public opinion turns against a dysfunctional system that fails to deliver." Together, these factors help create the conditions for populism, which rejects neoliberalism and the parties that enabled it, and also rejects politics-as-usual. This, argues Fraser, is the crisis of our times.

Fraser is not alone in identifying the economy as a contributing factor to populism's rise, or in describing circumstances in which extensive privatization works against the public good. For instance, Miller-Idriss notes a correlation between a population's economic precarity and its susceptibility to right-wing extremism, and Kauffman (chapter 5) indicates that the Women's March Inc.'s capacity to resist populism was hampered by its reliance on "specialized private firms or individual contractors," a practice typical of progressive nonprofits in the neoliberal era. Focusing on the

Tea Party, a U.S.-based, middle-class populist movement of libertarian Republicans and independents, White considers how the media amplify populist frames (chapter 1). After a cable news journalist called for capitalists to protest the financial bailout of homeowners in the wake of the 2008 financial crisis, news media constructed the Tea Party, claiming a "folk identity as populists even while it was explicitly pro-business and anti-poor."

White argues that rather than being a genuine populist movement, the Tea Party represents an instance of aggressive capitalism not unlike the populism portrayed by Fraser. Their populism, and anti-elitism, was performative rather than ideological, and was deployed, White writes, "as a way of framing a particular group of people (largely white Americans and, frequently, white men) as 'the people' . . . to whom we should pay attention." The fact that Tea Partiers are hardly "downtrodden" masses suggests that right-wing populism can often be an attempt to bolster the ruling class rather than displace it, as Moghadam warns in chapter 1. Key to this effort is the scapegoating of others, which sometimes involves falsely framing them as "elites."

Gender Performances

Contemporary right-wing populists often frame gender, and the search for gender equality, as the concern of elites and therefore at odds with the interests of "the people." They see feminist conceptions of gender as a threat to biological notions of sex, which underlie reactionary gender politics, writes Sabine Hark in chapter 2. The Right fights back by appropriating the term "gender" and tying it to "what people fear (globalization, the loss of jobs, houses, decent income, pensions, status, security)." The Right also "instrumentalize[s] gender as a signifier of how we are all governed," asserting that it is tantamount to totalitarianism. Hark argues that this strategy unites a motley agglomeration of "neoreactionary forces" and enables this coalition to present itself as the savior of "ordinary men and women," and to "reinforce racist demarcations" in a way that undermines the values of contemporary Western democracies. The Right therefore empties the term "gender" of content and manipulates it to create "an emotionally charged and increasingly racist opposition between 'the people' and 'the establishment.'" Gender becomes a speech act, or a performance, used for nefarious ends.

Populists perform gender in varied ways. Addressing their performance of masculinity, Amrita Basu observes in chapter 3 that most right-wing populists are aggressively masculine, displaying "sexual bravado," blatant homophobia, and crude identifications with stereotypical, working-class male behavior. "They feminize established elites to justify humiliating, denigrating, and bullying them," she writes, while also "depict[ing] historically disenfranchised racial and ethnic minorities as dangerously hyper-masculine." But India's prime minister Narendranath Modi is different, she argues. At times, he deploys male dominance and aggressive nationalism, flaunting his physique, which he compares to that of a wrestler. At other times he performs the role of the feminized, religious ascetic. As such, he projects "prototypical soft and feminine attributes" in ways resonant with the popular imagination of Gandhi, suggesting that he can replicate the latter's humility, as well as the "simplicity, unpretentiousness, and empathy for the quotidian indignities people suffer." Modi's success indicates that populist leaders do not draw on a common script, says Basu. It shows instead that "populist performances are most effective when they mine—and in the process rewrite—historical myths and memories."

Gender, of course, has also played a role as a mobilizing tool against populism. L. A. Kauffman's essay discusses the role of gendered resistance to the former U.S. president Donald Trump and the authoritarian populism he represents. The January 2017 Women's March was an explicitly feminist undertaking on a mass scale, with record-breaking grassroots participation. In chapter 5, Kauffman writes that women constituted "80 percent or more—of participants in every aspect of the sprawling decentralized resistance to Trump administration policies, whether . . . [in] the form of marching and rallying, engaging in grassroots lobbying, registering voters, or taking part in civil disobedience actions." In the first two years of its existence as a fledgling organization, Women's March Inc. built an intersectional feminist policy platform, mobilizing extensively on issues as varied as gun violence, the Muslim ban, and the appointment of Supreme Court justice Brett Kavanaugh. The Women's March also centered the leadership of women of color in crucial ways, even though its base was 70 percent white and consisted mainly of women who had relatively little activist history. While the Women's March Inc. faced organizational challenges that ultimately undermined its efforts to create a robust structure, Kauffman argues that this should not detract from its initial achievements. "Intersectional feminism," writes Kauffman, "had the potential to be not just the antithesis but a powerful antidote to the rise of authoritarian populism."

Organizing to Protect Democracy

How can we protect democracy from the threat of authoritarian right-wing populism? What is the relationship between grassroots organizing and activist work in established political parties? As Miller-Idriss notes in chapter 1, right-wing populism can take root within political parties, and seek to demolish democratic systems from within. When a strong-man declares he must step in to defend the "people" against internal and external threats—whether they are corrupt elites, or immigrants, or cultural change in general—then "other antidemocratic norms, values, beliefs and practices" are more likely to become mainstreamed. Democratic hall-marks like free and fair elections, freedom of the press, or systems of checks and balances are likely to be threatened. This is why (in "Organizing for Power") activist Heather Booth argues in chapter 6 that former U.S. president Donald Trump—a man who has consistently challenged the norms and values associated with liberal democracy—poses a grave threat to democracy along with "the forces that he represents."

Trump has emboldened the radical Right and furthered its influence within the Republican Party, and also in law enforcement agencies at the local level. Scot Nakagawa describes how white nationalism is infiltrating rural law enforcement agencies through organizations such as the Oath Keepers and the Three Percenters. Members of these organizations, often former veterans and first responders, are volunteering in fire departments and 911 services, filling the gaps left by budget cuts. "They're like Isis," Nakagawa comments in chapter 6. "They go where there are power voids." White nationalists, by pushing for extensive gun rights, are challenging the police's "monopoly on violence." They are becoming increasingly well organized, especially in the Western United States. Still, Nakagawa points out, "wherever there is an expression of hatred and authoritari-anism, then there is also resistance."

Indeed, Nakagawa, Booth, and Josephson emphasize the continued importance of community organizing—as a rela-tional practice, using techniques such as deep canvassing, and through institutions like the Midwest Academy, the

Industrial Areas Foundation, and the Highlander Center. As Josephson argues in chapter 6, "people build democracy together, and most of it takes local level, long-term organizing." It is this process of organizing, according to Booth, that will help shift us away from the current moment of authoritarian populism. "We'll turn this incredibly perilous time into a time of inspiration," she says. "And we'll look back and say remember when we organized, and we changed the world."

But what kind of democracy should we fight to protect? Moghadam argues that in the Middle East and North Africa, surveys reveal a preference for democracy over other forms of governance. But the people of this region "are certainly not in favor of a neoliberal capitalist democracy," she writes in chapter 1. What matters is that a political system meets their "socioeconomic interests and needs." In other words, "Electoral democracy and freedom of expression and association are not enough: democracy has to deliver to the population as a whole." Digital technologies are likely to play a role in that future. White argues that social media, which has contributed to the rise of post-truth politics, has also enabled formerly marginalized feminist voices, especially those of women of color, to have a greater impact on the public sphere. And, of course, technologies like Facebook and Twitter have already been used to mobilize against right-wing populism—witness the Arab Spring uprisings, Black Lives Matter, and the Women's March, which began with a Facebook post.

Taken as a whole, this interdisciplinary collection of essays reveals the dangers that populism poses to democracies and points the way forward. It also points to the need for further feminist analyses of populism, gender, and democracy. As Moghadam suggests, "All the pressing issues of our time—income and wealth inequality, capital's dominion over labor, militarism and war, racial and gender oppression, environmental degradation—are feminist issues"—and require a feminist solution. We hope this volume provokes readers to imagine how feminism can help us move beyond these perilous times and gesture toward a more just future.

Note

1. We began to conceptualize this project in 2016. The following year Sahar Abi-Hassan observed that "few studies" had thus far "made a comprehensive contribution to our understanding of the relationship between gender and populism" (2017, 426).

References

Abi-Hassan, Sahar. 2017. "Populism and Gender." In *The Oxford Handbook of Populism*, edited by Cristóbal Rovira Kaltwasser, Paul Taggart, Paulina Ochoa Espejo, and Pierre Ostiguy, 426–444. New York: Oxford University Press.

Blee, Kathleen M. 2008. *Women of the Klan: Racism and Gender in the 1920s*. Berkeley: University of California Press.

Corredor, Elizabeth S. 2019. "Unpacking 'Gender Ideology' and the Global Right's Antigender Countermovement." *Signs: Journal of Women in Culture and Society* 44 (3): 613–638. https://doi.org/10.1086/701171.

de la Torre, Carlos. 2017. "Populism and Democracy: Lessons from Latin America." *Seton Hall Journal of Diplomacy and International Relations* 18 (2): 33–48.

Dietze, Gabriel, and Julia Roth. 2020. *Right-Wing Populism and Gender: European Perspectives and Beyond*. New York: Columbia University Press.

Farris, Sara R. 2017. *In the Name of Women's Rights: The Rise of Femonationalism*. Durham: Duke University Press.

Fishman, Andrew. 2018. "Jair Bolsonaro Is Elected President of Brazil: Read His Extremist, Far-Right Positions in His Own Words." *The Intercept*, October 28, 2018. https://theintercept .com/2018/10/28/jair-bolsonaro-elected-president-brazil/.

Geva, Dorit. 2020. "A Double-Headed Hydra: Marine Le Pen's Charisma, between Political Masculinity and Political Femininity." *NORMA* 15 (1): 26–42. https://doi.org/10.1080/18902138.2019 .1701787.

Gill Peterson, Jules. 2021. "The Anti-Trans Lobby's Real Agenda," *Jewish Currents*, April 27, 2021. https://jewishcurrents.org/the -anti-trans-lobbys-real-agenda.

Graff, Agnieszka. 2014. "Report from the Gender Trenches: War against 'Genderism' in Poland." *European Journal of Women's Studies* 21 (4): 431–442. https://doi.org/10.1177/1350506814546091.

Graff, Agnieszka, Ratna Kapur, and Suzanna Danuta Walters, eds. 2019. "Gender and the Rise of the Global Right." Special issue, *Signs: Journal of Women in Culture and Society* 44, no. 3 (Spring). https://www.journals.uchicago.edu/toc/signs/2019/44/3.

Grattan, Laura. 2014. "Populism and the Rebellious Cultures of Democracy." In *Radical Future Pasts: Untimely Political Theory*, edited by Romand Coles, Mark Reinhardt, and George Shulman, 179–216. Lexington: The University Press of Kentucky.

———. 2020. "Populism, Race, and Radical Imagination #Feeling-TheBern in the Age of #BlackLivesMatter." In *Populism in Global Perspective: A Performative and Discursive Approach*, edited by Pierre Ostiguy, Francisco Panizza, and Benjamin Moffitt, 136–154. New York: Routledge.

Hirschmann, Nancy, J. 2021. "Populism and Protest." *Frontiers in Sociology* 5. https://doi.org/10.3389/fsoc.2020.619235.

Hobbes, Thomas. (1651) 1968. *Leviathan*. Harmondsworth: Penguin.

Hunter, James Davison. 1992. *Culture Wars: The Struggle to Define America*. New York: Basic Books.

Kimmel, Michael. 2017. *Angry White Men: American Masculinity at the End of an Era*. New York: Bold Type.

Kováts, Eszter, and Maari Põim. 2015. *Gender as Symbolic Glue: The Position and Role of Conservative and Far Right Parties in the Anti-gender Mobilizations in Europe.* Brussels: Foundation for European Progressive Studies and Friedrich-Ebert-Stiftung. https://library.fes.de/pdf-files/bueros/budapest/11382.pdf.

Laclau, Ernesto. 2005. *On Populist Reason.* New York: Verso.

Löffler, Marion, Russell Luyt, and Kathleen Starck. 2020. "Political Masculinities and Populism." *NORMA* 15 (1): 1–9. https://doi.org/10.1080/18902138.2020.1721154.

McKean, Benjamin L. 2016. "Toward an Inclusive Populism? On the Role of Race and Difference in Laclau's Politics." *Political Theory* 44 (6): 797–820.

Meadow, Tey. 2018. *Trans Kids: Being Gendered in the Twenty-First Century.* Oakland: University of California Press.

Mills, Charles, W. 1997. *The Racial Contract.* New York: Cornell University Press.

Moffitt, Benjamin. 2016. *The Global Rise of Populism: Performance, Political Style, and Representation.* Stanford, CA: Stanford University Press.

Mostov, Julie. 2021. "Populism Is Always Gendered and Dangerous." *Frontiers in Sociology* 5. https://doi.org/10.3389/fsoc.2020.625385.

Mouffe Chantal. 2005. "The 'End of Politics' and the Challenge of Right-Wing Populism." In *Populism and the Mirror of Democracy*, edited by Francisco Panizza, 50–71. New York: Verso.

———. 2018. *For a Left Populism.* New York: Verso.

Mudde, Cas. 2021. "Populism in Europe: An Illiberal Democratic Response to Undemocratic Liberalism (The Government and Opposition/Leonard Schapiro Lecture 2019)." *Government and Opposition*, 1–21. doi:10.1017/gov.2021.15.

Mudde, Cas, and Cristóbal Rovira Kaltwasser. 2017. *Populism: A Very Short Introduction.* New York: Oxford University Press.

Oxford Languages. 2016. "Word of the Year 2016." Oxford University Press. https://languages.oup.com/word-of-the-year/2016/.

Pateman, Carole. 1989. "'God Hath Ordained to Man a Helper': Hobbes, Patriarchy, and Conjugal Right." *British Journal of Political Science* 19 (4): 445–463.

Roth, Silke. 2018. "Introduction: Contemporary Counter-Movements in the Age of Brexit and Trump." *Sociological Research Online* 23 (2): 496–506.

Stein, Arlene. 2001. *The Stranger Next Door: The Story of a Small Community's Battle Over Sex, Faith, and Civil Rights*. Boston: Beacon Press.

Stern, Alexandra Minna. 2019. *Proud Boys and the White Ethnostate*. Boston: Beacon Press.

Urbinati, Nadia. 2019. "Political Theory of Populism." *Annual Review of Political Science* 22: 111–127. https://doi.org/10.1146/annurev -polisci-050317- 070753.

Wacquant, Loïc. 2012. "Three Steps to a Historical Anthropology of Actually Existing Neoliberalism." *Social Anthropology* 20 (1): 66–79. doi:10.1111/j.1469-8676.2011.00189.x.

Wallace-Wells, Benjamin. 2021. "How a Conservative Activist Invented the Conflict Over Critical Race Theory." *New Yorker*, June 18, 2021. https://www.newyorker.com/news/annals-of -inquiry/how-a-conservative-activist-invented-the-conflict-over -critical-race-theory.

Weyland, Kurt. 2018. Populism and authoritarianism. In *Routledge Handbook of Global Populism*, edited by Carlos de la Torre, 319–333. New York: Routledge.

Fragile Democracies
in a Post-Truth Era

KHADIJAH COSTLEY WHITE, CYNTHIA
MILLER-IDRISS, AND VALENTINE M. MOGHADAM

Democracy is under attack by right-wing populist move-ments that target elites, vulnerable populations, and the very nature of truth. How should feminists respond? The Insti-tute for Research on Women at Rutgers University hosted a panel with three leading scholars to discuss this perilous set of developments. We asked our three speakers, Khadi-jah Costley White (Journalism and Media Studies, Rutgers University–New Brunswick), Cynthia Miller-Idriss (School of Public Affairs and Education, American University), and Valentine M. Moghadam (Sociology and International Affairs, Northeastern University), to discuss challenges to contemporary democracies, including the populist devalua-tion of truth and attacks on expertise, and how they are joined with attacks on immigrants, women, and racial/ ethnic minorities. The following discussion, written in the event's aftermath, is based on that panel.

What Is Populism?

Cynthia: In its simplest definition, populism is a way of positioning ordinary people against corrupt elites. This is a rhetorical strategy, but it is also a schemata or way of thinking. It shapes the kinds of political tactics and frames that parties use to mobilize voters, as well as the ways in which those tactics are received, understood, and interpreted by ordinary people on the ground.

Most of my research focuses on the Far Right, which has exploited the growing appeal of anti-elite populist frames to mobilize antigovernment and anti-immigrant sentiments. Populism isn't limited to the Right, of course. As a rhetorical strategy or as a way of thinking, populism is evident across the political spectrum. But it has emerged as a popular tactic over the past decade or so among radical and Far Right parties across the globe, which has brought renewed attention to it in light of rising xenophobia and anti-immigrant sentiments. I call this kind of populism "populist nationalism." Populist nationalism takes the main populist framing of ordinary people against nefarious elites and broadens the threat to include others, such as immigrants, racial and religious minorities, the liberal Left, or multiculturalism itself. For populist nationalists, the pure people are at risk not only from corrupt elites but also from immigration and cultural change. Populist nationalists warn the people that they must be protected by a stronger state that can fight back against corrupt elites, government waste, corporate greed, and rising immigration, all at once.

The linking together of these themes—greedy and corrupt governments, corporate elites, and threatening immigration patterns—rests in part on discussions about how the economic exploitation of the Global South by global elites has created increasing waves of economic and conflict-driven migrant refugees to the North. The unchecked greediness of the multinational corporate sector, so the argument goes, has consequences for the stability of individual nations and the increasing numbers of refugees it must support. This kind of anti-immigrant argument appeals to individuals across the political spectrum who are concerned about corporate power or unchecked capitalism, which can have the effect of muddying the Far Right's ideological grounding and broadening their base of supporters. Populist nationalists suggest that a stronger state—even an undemocratic one—would be able to push back against multinational and transnational organizations and agencies, which ostensibly work against the interests of individual nations and their national citizens. We have seen the same kinds of arguments within the Far Right across Europe during the COVID-19 pandemic, for example, where coronavirus-shutdown protests become opportunities for the Far Right to undermine trust and confidence in the government and suggest that a stronger, authoritarian state would better protect the people, their economic livelihood, and their health.

This is where populism is at its most undemocratic. The people are seen as in need of protection from elites and from external others but also from their own choices. A more authoritarian leader or regime promises to protect them from themselves and secure choices on their behalf that will benefit the nation as a whole, even if it is not what individuals would have chosen for themselves. And these same kinds of populist frames can be used to carry a wide variety of other antidemocratic norms, values, beliefs, and practices into the mainstream, as populist nationalists challenge democratic hallmarks like free and fair elections, freedom of the press, or systems of checks and balances. Some Far Right movements intentionally seek to undermine democracy globally, through the use of disinformation campaigns, election interference, or attacks on the freedom of the press. But not all Far Right movements work against mainstream governments—in many countries, Far Right and populist nationalist political parties are working within the system to try to undermine from the inside. Parties thus campaign to be elected to parliamentary seats in order to dismantle or reduce the powers of the European Union, for example, or to force more mainstream parties to adopt positions like anti-immigration platforms in order to win back voters. These trends have made it harder for the public to differentiate between groups that once reflected the extreme fringe of political spectrums and groups that are in the mainstream conservative Right. While extreme groups like patriot militias and sovereign citizen groups make their antigovernment agendas clear, the election of Donald Trump has also shown that a candidate running on a mainstream party's platform can be successful by reinforcing anti-elite and antigovernment arguments, as expressed in the promise to "drain the swamp."

The conditions that lead to more receptivity to populist frames are varied, but one constant is a growing sense of insecurity or precarity. As lives in which stable incomes, predictable retirement, and reliable health insurance become less and less the reality for citizens, they become more susceptible to populist rhetoric that seeks to place the blame on others and seeks scapegoats for their plight. It is important to be clear that this in no way means that racist, xenophobic, anti-Semitic, Islamophobic, or other exclusionary and dehumanizing ideologies or behaviors should be excused or justified based on growing economic insecurity. White supremacy is an assumed, foundational premise to populist nationalist arguments that seek to exclude, deport, or otherwise ban entire populations from entering or remaining within a given nation's borders. In the same way, the racial makeup of the thousands of protesters who marched on state capitols in the United States in spring 2020 to protest state shutdown orders during the COVID-19 pandemic is notable. Antigovernment protesters were predominantly white, while COVID-19 deaths have disproportionately affected communities of color. It is not only economic vulnerability that mobilizes populist movements—racial dynamics and underlying white supremacist assumptions, even when unacknowledged, also play a key role.

Global Populism

Valentine: Right-wing populism is now a global phenomenon, present in the Global South as well as the Global North. It is not, however, new, given its long history in Russia and the United States and the deployment of populist rhetoric and policies of various ideological hues in Latin America and Europe. An even earlier manifestation was brilliantly analyzed as "Bonapartism" by Karl Marx, in *The Eighteenth Brumaire of Louis Bonaparte* ([1852] 1977). Vladimir Lenin used the term to describe the counterrevolutionary nature of the Russian bourgeoisie after the July 1917 crisis. The term "Bonapartist" came to be used more generally for a political movement that advocates an authoritarian centralized state with a strongman charismatic leader based on anti-elitist rhetoric and conservatism. In spring 1979, following the Iranian revolution, some Iranian leftists used the terms "populist" and "Bonapartist" to describe the new Islamic revolutionary state.

If earlier episodes of populism, often tinged with nativism, emerged from the contradictions of the transition from traditional to modern society during the early industrial era (e.g., displacements and exploitation), many studies describe the current wave as a backlash against the contradictions of neoliberal globalization, often blamed on elites or migrants or foreign countries. The profound deficits of what has become an oligarchic form of democracy have angered citizens across the globe and generated reaction on the Right as well as on the Left. The right-wing anti-elite rhetoric, however, masks policies and practices that, in fact, serve to consolidate the ruling capitalist class. Obvious examples are Trump's tax cuts for the rich and the soaring capital gains for the biggest shareholders in the stock market while so many Americans have suffered health crises and job losses. In another example, Turkey's president, Recep Tayyip Erdoğan, may pepper his speeches with references to "the Turkish people" and the "Muslim nation," but his economic policies and the many construction contracts issued by his government have favored the Islamic segment of the economic elites. Meanwhile, desecularization, an aggressive nationalism, and an antifeminist, patriarchal regression have occurred.

Indeed, in *Globalization and Social Movements: The Populist Challenge and Democratic Alternatives* (2020), I show that many Islamist governments and movements are part of the global right-wing populist panoply. They include Turkey's ruling AKP (Justice and Development Party) as well as the various offshoots of the Muslim Brotherhood in Arab countries, such as Morocco, Tunisia, and Jordan. Just as European populists mobilize against "the Muslim invasion," some Islamist movements, parties, and governments oppose "Western cultural invasion" and "alien" values, such as feminism, gay rights, and civil liberties. What they have in common is an emphasis on and valorization of family, religion, and what they perceive to be their own unitary culture. The implications for women's autonomy and rights are profound, as are the implications for the future of democracy.

Fortunately, in the MENA (Middle East and North Africa) region, feminist advocacy and activism are spreading and taking hold culturally. Even many believing Muslims support women's rights (although highly religious Muslims associated with Islamist parties generally oppose women's full equality in the family, along with abortion, gay equality, and equality of non-Muslim citizens). In the protest wave of 2019–2020, feminist activists joined youth and other citizens in Algeria, Egypt, Iraq, Lebanon, Morocco, Tunisia, and other countries, to protest incompetent or corrupt governments, economic difficulties, and the absence of democratic decision making.

It is important to note that right-wing populism is not the only worrisome development in the MENA region. Another culprit is external: invasions, economic sanctions, destabilization of states, or other violations of national sovereignty. These have done enormous damage to women, men, and children, and they usually result in right-wing backlashes against women and minorities, or in a stronger position for violent extremism. Pertinent examples are Iraq after the 2003 American invasion; Libya's chaos and site for human trafficking after the 2011 NATO invasion and grotesque death of Ghaddafi; the rise of the so-called Islamic State (IS/ISIS/Da'esh) following the destabilization of Syria. Algeria, Morocco, and Tunisia have been spared such undue international interference, which has enabled the feminist organizations in those countries to advance their agenda for women's equality and societal change. Tunisian feminism, in particular, was pivotal in enabling a peaceful and democratic outcome of the 2011 revolution.

American Populism and the Media

Khadijah: My research explores the relationship between American populism and the media. In my book *The Branding of Right-Wing Activism: The News Media and the Tea Party*

(2018) examining news discourses on the Tea Party, I examine at how race, gender, and truth play a role in the Tea Party's rise and some of the populist rhetoric that spurred it on. The Tea Party emerged in part as a story of populism as steeped in brand culture. I argue in my book that while there were indeed grassroots supporters of the Tea Party, it is best understood as a multifaceted, discursive signifier that helped attract voters, get media attention, and reinvent the Republican Party. In other words, it mostly functioned as a brand.

In the contemporary context, commerce, political action, and identity construction overlap within a competitive capitalist landscape. Brands are stories that are told about an object that allow a consumer to emotionally connect to it. In the process of branding, consumers do not evaluate the quality of the product as much as they value the way it makes them feel. Brands function as a cognitive shortcut that packages all those feelings, ideas, and sentiments invoked in the branding of a product in an easy, quickly recognizable way. Branding produces a context in which "facts are less influential in shaping public opinion"—it is a process that *aims* to supplant facts in exchange for sentiment.

I wanted to find out how media narratives constructed the Tea Party, and what that tells us about American politics as it overlaps with brand culture. Frequently, news reports described Tea Partiers as rebelling populists, even while the factual details seemed to undermine the rhetorical spectacle. Tea Partiers demanded that President Barack Obama deliver lower taxes when the federal tax rate was at its lowest in decades. Tea Partiers largely opposed the gains and policies of the American civil rights and women's movements, but Tea Party supporters still claimed the legacy of these social movements as part of their own activism.

The Tea Party itself was kicked off on live TV by Rick Santelli, a cable news reporter calling for "capitalists" to come and join him for a protest in Chicago. On *Fox News*, reporters advertised Tea Party events and urged other networks to report on the Tea Party, and a news anchor served as a headliner at a rally. In simultaneously promoting themselves through reporting on the Tea Party, reporters, pundits, and journalists became the co-producers, consumers, and creators of the Tea Party brand. The rise of the Tea Party was thus indicative of the impact of brand culture on journalism today, a snapshot of what is possible in a moment of political branding and journalism.

The news media allowed the Tea Party to claim a folk identity as populists even while it was explicitly probusiness and anti-poor. While the nineteenth-century Populist Party demanded a "redistribution of wealth," the twenty-first-century Tea Party leaders blamed the poor for their own economic circumstances. Research showed that Tea Partiers were actually wealthier and more educated than the rest of the population. But the news framing them as populists helped secure their narrative as part of the downtrodden— it helped validate and promote their brand. In the book, I discuss how the term "populism" was deployed as a way of framing a particular group of people (largely white Americans and, frequently, white men) as "the people." That is, the news descriptions of Tea Partiers as "populist" rely less on the notion that they are an organized group of Americans mobilized around a particular political ideology that resists the domination of a specific set of elites, and more on the idea that they are a certain *type* of American to whom we should pay attention. Conversely, antiwar, women's rights, and civil rights activists do not often get framed as "populist" in news narratives (even when they are explicitly anticapitalist and anticorporate).

In part, the news media helped promote populism as part of the Tea Party brand through their news narratives about the Tea Party that focused on class, race, and gender. As I argue in my book, people are more attracted to a brand when it resembles how they see themselves and their values, norms, behavior, or beliefs. In political branding, this often means drawing on powerful identities while often eclipsing their meaning or substance. For example, I point out that Tea Party leader Sarah Palin used the term "Mama Grizzlies" as a cognitive shortcut for referencing the conservative women candidates she supported. "Mama Grizzlies" invoked the idea of women (specifically, white women) fighting for their children in the political battleground the way that a mama bear would naturally (and violently) fight for the safety of her own cubs.

Ironically, a substantial number of Palin's Mama Grizzly candidates were not mothers at all. Still, the term "Mama Grizzly" was effective as an extension of the Tea Party's revolutionary populist brand because it functioned as a story that evoked feelings related to motherhood, softened anger and rage as self-defense, justified as maternal instinct any of the women candidates' potentially harsh political attacks on their competitors, and connected easily with people. In branding, race and gender help make a brand seem more human and amplify its emotional connection to consumers. In similar ways, the term "Tea Party" drew on historical notions of revolution, whiteness, populism, and domination to sell its own political brand, a frame repeated and legitimized through news coverage.

Populism, Democracies, and Post-Truth Politics

Khadijah: In a democracy, the rules and practices of government should maximally benefit the people that elected leaders are supposed to represent—that is, building and developing policies for the public are key to a functioning democracy. In this framework, relaying information that helps the public better understand policy is a vital function. Journalists gather and convey this information to help the public better navigate, communicate, and react to the actions of their leaders and hold them accountable.

But in a brand culture, the media tend to focus on how a politician makes one feel, not on the impact of policies. One's identity connects to politics and reinforces those feelings. People in a brand culture are expected to vote their tastes and not necessarily for specific political outcomes; that is, politics is consumption in a brand culture and citizenship becomes a lifestyle that emphasizes individualism and self-fulfillment. Politics in a brand culture is a form of self-expression and identity rather than a tool of power and governance. In this way, a political brand culture often stands in conflict with the goals of democracy, which aims for a mutually beneficial society focused on best serving the public interest.

Brand culture is a fertile ground for the breeding of post-truth. "Post-truth" rose as a widely used term in the first two decades of the twenty-first century, becoming Oxford's word of the year in 2016. The definition of "post-truth" according to the *Oxford Dictionaries* is "relating to or denoting circumstances in which objective facts are less influential in shaping public opinion than appeals to emotion and personal belief" (Oxford Languages 2016). Since it requires the persuasive framing and consumption of "alternative facts" (as presidential senior adviser Kellyanne Conway so famously put it in a 2017 news interview), branding is a key mechanism of a post-truth society. It renders substantive differences between two products (or candidates) as less important than the way the objects (or people) make you feel. Information becomes important not because of its veracity, but because of the emotion it evokes. In other words, post-truth sells.

Post-truth marks the "weakening social position of experts, the rise of partisan-divided trust in facts, statistics, and journalism, and the politicization of science," in which various actors "vie for public attention, legitimacy, and power" (Waisbord 2018, 1870). James Ball explains that these post-truth shifts have proven financially profitable in producing misinformation industries abroad and for corporations like Facebook and YouTube (2017). Post-truth "regimes" are produced through "truth markets," managed and controlled by data-driven businesses (Harsin 2015, 332). The profitability of misinformation and audience segmentation help drive post-truth.

The way post-truth is discussed today differs from earlier historical periods in which researchers tracked and analyzed the manipulated flows of information in society. While the twentieth century saw the erection of a societal effort to establish science and empiricism as a definitive arbiter of truth in order to counter misinformation, post-truth in the early twenty-first century is defined by the dissolution of that effort and the refutation of science and facts themselves as the result of flawed ideological processes. It is marked by a shift in technology that allows less control of media narratives by elites, experts, and other authorities.

The result of post-truth is a crisis in which science, expertise, facts, and reality can be undermined to our collective detriment. Vaccine denialism is one example of a post-truth conviction with dire consequences. Another example of the consequences of a post-truth position is Donald Trump's response to the 2020 global coronavirus pandemic. "You have 15 people, and the 15 within a couple of days is going to be down to close to zero," the American president confidently told an eager crowd in February, despite scientific predictions of exponential rates of infection and casualties (Chait 2020). As I write this in September 2020, over 200,000 people have died from COVID-19, and more than seven million people have tested positive for the virus.

Scholars examining post-truth ideology in American politics look at how the modern surge of available information affects our democracy; some see the lapse of a belief in shared truths as a failure of civic engagement, public service, and democratic institutions. My research on the Tea Party provides an example of how news discourse shapes these ideas through the circulation of narratives that minimize or even contradict the facts; consequently, erosion in faith and trust in key institutions heightens the importance of identity and prioritizes one's sense of self in modern politics. Additionally, the rise of postracial and postfeminist rhetorics at the same time as "post-truth" discourses suggests that race and gender are inextricably tied to the truths we value and understand; in other words, it seems that race and gender have an impact on and shape the post-truth landscape of American politics.

Cynthia: The same conditions that lend themselves to receptivity to populist frames create vulnerability to misinformation, disinformation, and conspiracy theories. Populism has not caused the rise in conspiratorial thinking and conspiracy theories, but anti-elite frames have certainly helped undermine expertise and authority in ways that may make people more receptive to alternative sources of purported knowledge or expertise.

The situation is exacerbated by new ecosystems of online communication, especially social media, which allow the rapid creation and spread of conspiracy theories in ways that further destabilize people's sense of truth, fact, and appropriate response. Conspiracy theories are especially popular around events that produce great uncertainty, such as volatile elections or political assassinations. But they are also rampant among long-festering crises, such as climate change and global warming, where a wide variety of conspiracy theories consistently undermines scientific evidence. The COVID-19 pandemic is one such example. Indeed, as I write this, while still under my region's shelter-in-place orders, it is hard to imagine a more pressing moment to engage the issue of post-truth politics than in the height of a global pandemic whose preventive policy responses are hampered by local populations' resistance to scientific expertise—such as the effectiveness of masks—and to government mandates to shelter in place.

Conspiracy theories become more popular during times of uncertainty because they offer what seems to be a clear explanation of the inexplicable that people are experiencing. The health insecurity and immediate economic crisis brought on by COVID-19 provide a clear case. But the virus and its broader impacts come on the heels of uncertainty brought on by a steady erosion of well-being for many individuals across the world amid uncertain labor markets and rising inequality. White and male grievance is also central to the radicalization and mobilization of white men in particular and to Far-Right backlash against feminism, science, and gender studies. The political context also contributes to cultural shifts that make populations more susceptible to conspiracy theories. Political leadership that espouses "alternative facts" or reinforces conspiracy theories helps to legitimize conspiracies that might have seemed far-fetched. And underlying racism, anti-Semitism, and Islamophobia can make some whites more receptive to white supremacist conspiracy theories about the purported threat posed by demographic change or immigration.

Misinformation and conspiracy theories are dangerous for democracy for many reasons. One is that they are effective tools for mainstreaming Far-Right ideas. That is, even when the conspiracy itself is not adopted by the mainstream, key elements can take hold, leading to increased anti-Semitism, for example, even if individuals reject the actual conspiracy of a George Soros–funded global "cabal" of Jews orchestrating migrant caravans. Increased bias or suspicion can evolve in ways that individuals may not even be fully aware of. Conspiracy theories also help polarize by clearly establishing "us" versus "them" in ways that are consistent with the same kind of populist nationalist framing discussed earlier.

Valentine: The concept of "post-truth politics" is commonly associated with the Trump/Pence regime in the United States, but misinformation, disinformation, and outright lies are not new to U.S. politics (or to British politics, or those of many other states). Nor is the post-truth era tied exclusively to the recent wave of right-wing populism. The long history of such propaganda predates the post–World War II era, but I would include the disinformation about Iran's constitutionally elected prime minister Mohammad Mosaddegh, who was overthrown in a U.S.- and UK-aided coup in August 1953. Mossadegh, who in fact had a fraught relationship with Iran's communist party (the Tudeh Party) and very much disliked the Soviet Union, was called a communist puppet, although his real "crime" was to nationalize Iran's oil industry.

Conspiracy theories and practices are not new, as they have been used extensively by liberal democracies. The conspiracy against the progressive-populist Congolese leader Patrice Lumumba derailed Congo's progressive political development. Lumumba was seized, tortured, and executed in a 1961 coup supported by Belgium and the United States, while the United Nations did nothing to prevent or oppose it. Disinformation and outright lies by the United States were pervasive during the Vietnam War, after the Afghan revolution of April 1978 and throughout its internationalized civil conflict in the 1980s, and of course throughout the 2003 U.S.–UK invasion and occupation of Iraq. These political realities tend to be forgotten, obscured, or denied by politicians, media pundits, and even political scientists. It seems that raison d'état trumps truth far too often. Fortunately, progressive movement organizations and media have emerged to challenge the conspiracies and lies, although they often struggle to be heard.

Populist Mobilizations Around Gender, Sexuality, Race, and Ethnicity

Valentine: The gender dynamics of populism are multifaceted, given that there are left-wing as well as right-wing varieties of populism. Some right-wing populist parties in Europe, for example, have women leaders. In any given country, there will be women attracted to right-wing populism, whether those parties are Islamist, secularist, Christian (e.g., Poland and Hungary), or Jewish (in Israel). Right-wing populist movements enjoy female support, but so do nationalist and religio-political movements. As with populism and its varieties, nationalism appears versatile and varied, with left-wing and right-wing, and pro- and antifeminist varieties. The rise of religious fundamentalisms in the 1980s—Christian, Islamic, Jewish, Hindu—generated a large body of feminist scholarship on the vexed relationship between feminism and religious-nationalist movements. In a 1994 edited volume, my collaborators and I documented those movements in Muslim-majority countries of the Middle East, North Africa, South Asia, and Sub-Saharan Africa, as well as in the U.S., Israel, and India. Those studies are relevant to the present discussion of right-wing populism and its gender dynamics because they reveal a history of women's attraction to and involvement in right-wing politics and some underlying reasons: economic displacement or anxieties, disillusionment with the cultural politics of secularism and liberal feminism, support for the traditional sexual division of labor, and effective political manipulation.

Both Islamist and European right-wing populists evince an aversion to certain cultural changes. In the same way that Germany's Alternative für Deutschland voters cited threats to "the German language and culture," many Muslims vote for Islamist parties to protect and preserve their culture and religion. And in the same way that many Muslims feel that Islam is under threat, right-wing populists in Poland and Hungary argue that "Christian Europe" is in danger of being overrun by Muslim immigrants and refugees who cannot or will not assimilate. The spate of jihadist murders in Europe in recent years has only added fuel to the fire.

Women who support right-wing populist parties or leaders—such as the 53 percent of white American women voters who cast their ballots for Trump in the 2016 presidential election or the 54 percent of Turkish women who voted for Erdoğan in 2011—may be homemakers who find security in the traditional sexual division of labor. But not all right-wing populist parties oppose gender equality and sexual rights. In many western European countries, they rail against immigrant communities where women wear burqas or eschew employment, or where families do not allow their daughters to attend swimming classes. A certain "femonationalism" invokes women's rights to stigmatize Muslim men (Farris 2017); Keskinen discusses right-wing Finnish "white border guard femininities" that draw on both traditional definitions of femininity and "liberal understandings of gender equality" (2018, 161). Cultural clashes and fear of crime may generate votes for right-wing populists, but also verbal and often physical attacks on immigrants, migrants, and refugees.

Cynthia: Populist nationalists mobilize broadly around issues of gender, sexuality, race and ethnicity. Race and ethnicity are foundational to populist nationalist anti-immigration and anti-Islam frames across Europe and North America, for example, whether that is through political rhetoric that dehumanizes immigrants with language about "shithole" countries or more general anti-immigration frames that depict migrants and refugees as diseased or dirty, or as invaders who pose an existential threat to the well-being of the nation and its citizens. The global "Great Replacement" conspiracy theory that has motivated recent white supremacist terrorists, such as the Christchurch and El Paso attackers, is fundamentally rooted in a fear of demographic change and multicultural societies—which are deemed an existential threat to white civilizations.

The issue of sexuality and gender has become somewhat more complicated. On the one hand, traditional populist nationalists call for women's return to "traditional" roles as wives, homemakers, and mothers. Women are seen as producers of the nation and its future soldiers, and are charged with maintaining traditional, Christian households, home-schooling children, nurturing and feeding families, and supporting their breadwinning husbands. These frames have long histories in nationalist and Far-Right movements, but also have modern forms, some of which are promoted by women who refer to themselves as "tradwives," calling for a return to a 1950s-style fantasy of gendered household division of labor and responsibilities. As Miranda Christou (2019, 2020) has argued based on qualitative research with Far-Right groups, women often play a key role in supporting and perpetuating misogynistic frameworks and hegemonic forms of masculinity. Gender itself, in other words, is not a protective factor against misogyny or hierarchical views of sex and gender, or against the Far Right more broadly.

On the other hand, some populist nationalist and Far-Right parties in Europe in particular have increased their base of voter support by using language about protecting women and the LGBTQ+ community from the threat of Sharia law if immigration and demographic change are not stopped. Such platforms claim LGBTQ+ and women's rights as part of "Western" values and position them against nefarious others, immigrants, and religious minorities who the Far Right claims would threaten those rights and values. By claiming frames that have traditionally fallen within leftist ideology—the promotion of rights for sexual minorities, women, and transgender communities—the Far Right has been able to win some voters away from the Left.

Khadijah: Typically, people tend to separate questions of race and gender from issues of truth in governance. They frame "postrace" and "postfeminist" discourses as a sign of societal *progress*, even as they raise alarms about the hazards of a post-truth democracy. One writer in *The Atlantic* argues that a "'post-feminist' perception of gender equality [represents] a notion that women are somehow running the world and that sexism towards women no longer exists" (Krischer 2017). Postfeminism also opens up less stringent ideas about gender, sexuality, and femininity, marked by an embrace of fashions, styles, occupations, and roles that had been viewed as oppressive by earlier feminist traditions. In a similar way, postrace (or the postracial era) signals that race and racism are no longer major social obstacles. President Barack Obama's 2008 electoral victory signals for some the end of racism in America. In the view of those who celebrate postfeminism and postrace, we have entered an era that liberates women and racially marginalized people from the restrictive rules, outdated social mores, and limitations on their choices imposed by their race or gender identity.

Yet gender and race (and class) were always implicitly (and sometimes, explicitly) a part of journalistic narratives about politics. Race and gender—or, rather, postrace and postfeminist politics—helped drive the sensationalism and circulation of Tea Party news.

The rise of postracial and postfeminist rhetorics alongside post-truth in the landscape of American politics suggests an important relationship between identity and how we configure truth. In part, branding is a key mechanism of post-truth. Branding allows for difference to stand in for oppression and equity—it emphasizes diversity while minimizing oppression. As identity gets deployed in political brands to create stories that attract consumers and supporters, it also displaces a public focus on collective experience and marginalization.

Post-truth de-emphasizes a centralized truth and instead asserts the importance of subjectivity and individual experience. Similarly, Darrel Enck-Wanzer writes that in postrace the "structural relevance of race is underscored through the neoliberal fantasy of personal responsibility" (2011, 26). In her writing on postfeminism, Angela McRobbie defines it as the "undoing of feminism" and an active process by which the feminist gains of the 1970s and 1980s come to be undermined" through the language of freedom and choice (2004, 255). The "truth" of race and gender in a post-truth landscape is disseminated through new forms of public communication that are more decentralized, participatory, and dynamic, but are also heavily influenced by neoliberal ideas that frame identity as part of one's brand—a result of self-expression rather than collective world building, of sentiment and affect rather than social movements.

Postfeminism and postracism signal the continuing influence of racial and gender oppression and subordination, not its waning significance. That is, we arrive at postrace and postfeminism because of previous failures (or refusals) to examine ongoing structural and systemic disparities and barriers that subjugate people based on race and gender. In other words, a narrative of postrace/postracism and postfeminism requires us to ignore facts which show that women are still compensated, promoted, and valued less than their male counterparts, or that Black people are still more poverty-stricken, policed, prosecuted, and insecure in terms of food and housing than their white peers. We ignore the facts of racism and sexism and cling to narratives of progress that make us *feel* better, even if they are more symbolic than real.

The Future through a Feminist Lens

Cynthia: I would argue that several things need to happen if we are going to reduce the polarization that is undermining democracies and democratic practices around the world. In order for a feminist lens to be effective in this process, such a lens would need to do at least four things. First, we need to work to challenge the continual undermining of academic and scientific expertise, the promotion of "alternative facts," and the idea that empirical evidence is just one ideological frame among many. These must be effectively challenged if we are ever going to address the rise of misinformation and disinformation. This includes responding to attacks on the academy and related organizations as well as on individual scholars.

Challenging the undermining of expertise also means developing coherent strategies for how to deal with fake news, which will get worse as technology improves and deep fake videos make it nearly impossible to detect what is real and what is not. This includes continual promotion and assertion of clear and respected sources of legitimacy. It means being clear, transparent, and open about our own biases, sources of funding and goals as they relate to our own research and being continually reflective on objectivity, subjectivity, and the assertion of facts. We need effective, empirically driven strategies that can undermine conspiracy theories and conspiratorial thinking.

Second, for a feminist lens to be effective at reducing polarization, it must be truly and authentically intersectional. This means educating ourselves and our communities about the historical legacies of both white supremacy and male supremacy for the ways in which they have foundationally shaped public policies and practices across the globe. This includes the legacies of colonialism and slavery and suffrage and structural racism, but also local injustices. Who could historically get a credit card, and who could get a mortgage in which neighborhood? Who was allowed to marry and who was not? Who had the power to earn an income that could lead to their family's security and inherited wealth for the generations to come? How did decades upon decades of economic insecurity and precarity affect the physical bodies and health of communities of color? Again, the disproportionate impact that COVID-19 has had on people of color in the United States alone is evidence of what legacies of racial disparities in health and access to health care mean in a time of crisis.

Third, a feminist lens can be most effective at reducing polarization if it is not just reactive but also proactive. We cannot continue to respond to developments as they occur; we must develop serious preventive and inoculation-based interventions that see polarization and rising extremism as the public health crises that they are. Children and adults need continually updated knowledge on how to recognize misinformation and disinformation, propaganda and manipulation, fake news, and conspiracy theories. We can recognize and challenge the ways that shelter-in-place orders and school shutdowns have created terrible outcomes in patterns of increased domestic violence and uneven burdens of domestic labor that leave mothers heavily responsible for home-schooling and household tasks. But we also need to call on all parents and caregivers to be more alert to the heightened risks of online radicalization and extreme polarization in the now almost entirely online world that youth and adults inhabit. Efforts spent in one area of the crisis do not preclude active engagement in other aspects.

Finally, a feminist lens can be effective at countering polarization if it is willing to challenge models of success that prioritize narrow metrics related to the economy as measures of whether a society is thriving. We have to understand that human development is not just one priority among many; it is the most essential feature of a thriving society. What does economic success mean if we don't have citizen well-being, societal empathy and caring, and mental health? It is clear that in several of the world's democracies with women at the helm—such as New Zealand—we are seeing a different kind of focus on human development and citizens' well-being, instead of measuring a nation's success based only on gross national product and economic gains.

This does not mean that empathy, caring, and well-being are the exclusive domain of feminist approaches to politics or that there is some sort of fixed or immutable gendered connection to more caring, empathic approaches. But if a feminist lens can bring new kinds of leadership, it would be a welcome change from generations of focus on economic development and corporate power at the expense of economic security, safety, and citizen well-being, especially for the most marginalized groups. I don't know if that will be enough to reverse rising polarization, but it would certainly be a place to start.

Valentine: Can feminists help bring about a more robust form of democracy? Arruzza, Bhattacharya, and Fraser (2019) have called for "a feminism for the 99%," which provides a Marxist-feminist critique of contemporary political, economic, and cultural arrangements. Recent years have seen several critiques of liberal feminism and its offshoots, including corporate, neoliberal, business, and imperial feminism. Feminist critics note that in the United States, what is needed is not a "lean in" feminism, or one that approves of more military spending and an aggressive foreign policy, but a *social feminism* for those who have been left behind, notably the mothers in precarious employment without decent childcare or health care, and those young women (and men) whose only real option in life is to join the military and fight in some foreign country they likely could not find on a map (which also points to the deficits of public schooling and the media).

The mission of the new Feminist Foreign Policy Project, which was created in 2018 by socialist feminists in and outside the academy, with the support of Code Pink: Women for Peace, echoes that of the *Manifesto for the 99%* but with a greater focus on the need for diplomacy and peace. It opposes economic sanctions, destabilization of states, and militarism. Rather than using development aid to support private contractors from donor countries, or using taxpayer money to build walls, a feminist foreign policy would insist that high-income governments invest in the social and physical infrastructure of poorer countries and help expand decent work, so that women, men, and children could live secure, healthy, and dignified lives in their own countries.

Surveys in the MENA region find that most citizens prefer democracy to any other political system, but they associate democracy largely with its capacity to meet people's socioeconomic interests and needs. MENA citizens are certainly not in favor of a neoliberal capitalist democracy; rather, they appear to favor a robust social democracy. There is also survey evidence that the establishment of liberal or electoral democracy and freedom of expression and association in the wake of the Arab Spring has not been enough to satisfy citizens' aspirations and needs—democracy must deliver to the population as a whole. Indeed, the danger in a new democracy like Tunisia is that the inability of democratic governance to deliver social rights and economic well-being could undermine people's confidence in democracy there and across the region. Tunisian feminists are aware of the risks, and for that reason they oppose austerity and call for a robust welfare state that also protects the civil, political, and social rights of all women.

All the pressing issues of our time—income and wealth inequality, capital's dominion over labor, militarism and war, racial and gender oppression, environmental degradation— are feminist issues. What is needed, therefore, is—at the very least—a *social feminism* that supports economic justice and wealth redistribution and stands in solidarity with striking teachers, factory workers, and minority groups; a feminism that works with young people for climate justice and tough environmental regulations; a *transnational social feminism* that opposes militarism and war and works with women's groups around the world to help end violence against women and all forms of sexual harassment and abuse—whether in the United States or Central America or sub-Saharan Africa.

Khadijah: The shifts in technology that typify a post-truth society have opened up spaces for marginalized people, particularly women and especially women of color. Ideas and theories about identity have frequently been dominated by majoritarian voices, constructing white and male experts as objective authorities through the discourse and methods of scientific knowledge. Using social media spaces like Twitter and Facebook, marginalized people can find a following and correct or otherwise respond to professional media discourses and representations.

The digitally circulated visibility of racism and sexual assault asserts the truth of sexism and racism. #MeToo and Black Lives Matter have dominated the national public sphere, resulting in policy and cultural shifts related to employment and workplace practices (for #MeToo) and policing, budgets, and prison abolition (for #BLM). Other similar kinds of social media discourses are able to challenge the "truth" of earlier eras that demanded the denial and minimization of this oppression (e.g., hashtags like #SolidarityIsForWhiteWomen to criticize the marginalization of women of color in white women's activism, or #OscarsSoWhite to highlight the lack of recognition given to Black actors and filmmakers).

Waisbord (2018) observes that new technocratic regimes have shifted information and knowledge flows and produced "counter-epistemic communities" that contest hegemonic accounts of reality, particularly reductive neoliberal ideas about race and gender that reduce identities to individualist choices and modes of expression.

Post-truth is not just about the lack of an authority, but also the crisis of authority itself vis-à-vis all the ways elites maintain regimes of power through discrimination and exclusion. This means pushing back at the methods, the data, and the very idea of research and facts as we understand them. As Patricia Hill Collins explains, Black feminist thought suggests another "path to the universal truths" that relies on the specificity of subjectivity and shared experience (2000, 269). In this way, a feminist lens—in particular, a Black feminist lens that centers oppression and inequality in its approach to societal analysis and critique—can help reshape a post-truth society in regard to epistemological innovation, inquiry, and validation.

References

Arruzza, Cinzia, Tithi Bhattacharya, and Nancy Fraser. 2019.
A Feminism for the 99%: A Manifesto. London: Verso Books.

Ball, James. 2017. *Post-Truth: How Bullshit Conquered the World*.
London: Biteback.

Chait, Jonathan. 2020. "Trump: I Was Right, Coronavirus Cases
'Will Go Down to Zero, Ultimately.'" *New York Magazine*.
April 28, 2020. https://nymag.com/intelligencer/2020/04/trump
-coronavirus-cases-will-go-down-to-zero-ultimately.html.

Christou, Miranda. 2019. "The Fragile, Toxic Masculinity of White
Supremacy." Centre for the Analysis of the Radical Right Insight.
September 23, 2019. https://www.radicalrightanalysis.com/2019
/09/23/the-fragile-toxic-masculinity-of-white-supremacy/.

———. 2020. "#TradWives: Sexism as a Gateway to White
Supremacy." Centre for the Analysis of the Radical Right
Insight. March 23, 2020. https://www.radicalrightanalysis.com
/2020/03/23/tradwives-sexism-as-gateway-to-white-supremacy/.

Costley White, Khadijah. 2018. *The Branding of Right-Wing Activism:
The News Media and the Tea Party*. Oxford: Oxford University Press.

Enck-Wanzer, Darrel. 2011. "Barack Obama, the Tea Party, and the
Threat of Race: On Racial Neoliberalism and Born Again
Racism." *Communication, Culture, and Critique* 4 (1): 23–30.
https://doi.org/10.1111/j.1753-9137.2010.01090.x.

Farris, Sara. 2017. *In the Name of Women's Rights: The Rise of Femonationalism*. Durham, NC: Duke University Press.

Fraser, Nancy. 2013. "How Feminism Became Capitalism's
Handmaiden—and How to Reclaim It." *The Guardian*,
October 13, 2013. https://www.theguardian.com/commentisfree
/2013/oct/14/feminism-capitalist-handmaiden-neoliberal.

Harsin, Jayson. 2015. "Regimes of Posttruth. Post-Politics, and
Attention Economies." *Communication, Culture and Critique* 8
(2): 327–333.

Hill Collins, Patricia. 2000. *Black Feminist Thought: Knowledge, Consciousness, and the Politics of Empowerment.* New York: Routledge.

Keskinen, Suvi. 2018. "The 'Crisis' of White Hegemony, Neonationalist Femininities, and Antiracist Feminism." *Women's Studies International Forum* 68:157–163.

Krischer, Hayley. 2017. "Are Girls Really Living in a 'Post-Feminist' World?" *The Atlantic*, July 12, 2020. https://www.theatlantic.com/education/archive/2017/07/everyday-sexism-in-a-post-feminist-world/533241/.

Marx, Karl. (1852) 1977. *The Eighteenth Brumaire of Louis Bonaparte.* In *Karl Marx: Selected Writings*, edited by David McLellan. Oxford: Oxford University Press.

McRobbie, Angela. 2004. "Post-Feminism and Popular Culture," *Feminist Media Studies* 4 (3): 255–264. https://doi.org/10.1080/1468077042000309937.

———. 2009. *The Aftermath of Feminism: Gender, Culture and Social Change.* London: Sage Publications.

Miller-Idriss, Cynthia. 2019. "The Global Dimensions of Populist Nationalism." *The International Spectator* 54, no. 2 (May): 17–34.

———. 2020. *Hate in the Homeland: The New Global Far Right.* Princeton, NJ: Princeton University Press.

Miller-Idriss, Cynthia, and Hilary Pilkington. 2019. *Gender and the Radical and Extreme Right: Mechanisms of Transmission and the Role of Educational Interventions.* New York: Routledge Press.

Moghadam, Valentine M., ed. 1994. *Identity Politics and Women: Cultural Reassertions and Feminisms in International Perspective.* Boulder, CO: Westview Press.

———. 2020. *Globalization and Social Movements: The Populist Challenge and Democratic Alternatives.* Lanham, MD: Rowman and Littlefield.

Moghadam, Valentine M., and Gizem Kaftan. 2019. "Right-Wing Populism North and South: Varieties and Gender

Dynamics." In *Women's Studies International Forum*, 75 (July–August).

Oxford Languages. 2016. "Word of the Year 2016." https://languages .oup.com/word-of-the-year/2016/.

Waisbord, Silvio. 2018. "Truth Is What Happens to News: On Journalism, Fake News, and Post-Truth." *Journalism Studies* 19 (13): 1866–1878.

2

Dispossession

*Gender and the Construction of Us /
Them Dichotomies*

SABINE HARK

Many nations have recently witnessed the rise of right-wing populist parties and dramatic shifts in the existing balance of power. As nationalistic, illiberal, and authoritarian forces become ascendant, it is tempting to argue that a new "International" of the Right has come into being. This International seems to take the form of a radically polarizing populism, together with authoritarianism or reactionary nationalism or both. It is characterized by racism; islamophobia; anti-Semitism; hatred of women, feminists, and LGBTIQ* people; and also, at times, attacks against the academic discipline of gender studies. This chapter focuses on the allegation that the scholarly study of gender threatens the natural and divine order of the sexes, heterosexual marriage, the family, and indeed the very foundation of Western society.

Interestingly, women authors, journalists, and scholars who describe themselves as feminists are among gender studies' most ferocious critics. The German author Gabriele Kuby is one of them. On her personal website Kuby presents herself as a trained sociologist speaking on the "global sexual revolution and Christian spirituality" (Kuby n.d.). Internationally, she is often introduced as Germany's leading sociologist of gender. She explains that her conversion to the Catholic faith in 1997 "opened her eyes for the dangers of the sexual revolution" (Kuby). Kuby presents her insights from this revelation in her book, *The Global Sexual Revolution: Destruction of Freedom in the Name of Freedom* (2015).

Internationally, Kuby's book is extensively distributed, often by Catholic presses, with translations financed by the Holy See. It has been sent at no cost to hundreds, maybe thousands, of politicians worldwide. The book's main argument illustrates four of the defining elements of an authoritarian, ultimately radically antidemocratic worldview: (1) the portrayal of society in terms of friend/foe dichotomies, (2) the language of control and usurpation, (3) the use of emotional appeals, and (4) aggressive mobilization.

Throughout her writing Kuby fervently fights against the alleged totalitarian ideology of "gender and LGBTIQ* demands," which seek to destroy the natural, divine, dignified order of things and people. She willfully misinterprets gender as a situational, episodic choice of lifestyle, a sort of "stylish makeup for the day." She insists that this ultralibertarian notion of gender is enforced on all people, especially on "innocent children." Likewise, she frames reproductive freedom as antinatural and a fundamental threat to social order. In sum, Kuby uses "gender" like an empty basket into which one can throw everything considered dangerous. Gender thus comes to stand for abortion, pedophilia, fornication, sodomy, or even euthanasia and eugenics. Most consistently, gender is used as a code for "moral degeneration" and the decline of Western civilization.

Kuby is not alone but one of many engaged in global attacks against gender and gender studies. Her ideas echo those of former Pope Benedict who lauded her as "a brave fighter against the ideologies that ultimately lead to the destruction of mankind" (quoted in Kuby n.d.). Her ideas also resonate extremely well with the convictions of current Pope Frances. Gender theory, Frances claims, is the "name of a new world war for the destruction of marriage" (Osborne 2016). In postcommunist countries, some bishops even claim that gender ideology is a far greater danger than National Socialism and communism put together.

The idea of gender as ideology goes back to the 1990s. In 1995 the Vatican argued that gender is nothing other than a code word for homosexuality, and references to it should therefore be eliminated from the United Nations Non-Governmental Organizations' Platform on the Status of Women. That same year, at the UN Conference on Women in Beijing, several UN member-states under the guidance of the Vatican sought to expunge the word "gender" from the Platform for Action and to replace it with the notion of "sex." In 2004 the Roman Catholic Family Council, then under the leadership of Joseph Ratzinger who would later become Pope Benedict, warned against the idea of gender as a threat to the family and to biblical authority (Ratzinger and Amato 2004). In subsequent years these ideas have traveled through-out the world in ways that document the global political power of the Vatican.

Judith Butler (2019) has recently pointed out that renewed papal support for the fight against gender may be encouraging bishops to escalate the campaign against gender ideology into an international project that crosses hemispheres. In the Global South, this campaign has affected elections in Colombia, Mexico, Costa Rica, and Brazil. The right-wing president of Brazil, Jair Bolsonaro, gave an inaugural speech in early January 2019 that contained a commitment to eradicate "gender ideology in the schools" (quoted in Butler 2019). Subsequently, he has sought to replace school-based sex education with a curriculum that enforces the idea of binary gender difference.

This attack on so-called gender ideology occurred in parts of Europe too. In October 2019, Hungary eliminated gender studies from its list of approved master's programs. Due to continuous government pressure, Central European University, known for its internationally renowned gender program, decided to relocate from Budapest to Vienna. In France, an elementary school textbook called *ABCD de l'Égalité* (ABCD of Equality) was introduced in 2014, a year after the successful legal battle for same-sex marriage. It offered students a way to think about the difference between biological sex and cultural gender. After massive protests by Catholic parents and Muslim families, the textbook was withdrawn.

These are just a few examples of the impact of a very powerful global network that includes the Holy See and conservative Catholic groupings, religious and lay conservative nongovernmental organizations worldwide, Evangelical Free Churches, pro-life movements, and nationalist-authoritarian parties and governments.[1] They explicitly oppose "gender," "gender theory," "gender ideology," or simply "genderism," and they all maintain more or less strong connections with movements on the racist, antidemocratic spectrum.

In the German-speaking world, polemics against gender in general and gender studies in particular began in the mid-2000s. Anti-Genderismus (antigenderism) has since become a common denominator for a diverse set of actors within the German ethnonationalist, right-wing, authoritarian, chauvinist, aggressively heteronormative, and racist political spectrum.[2] Attacks on gender studies and so-called gender ideology are also recurrent in mainstream media, often combined with anti-Islamic sentiments. They occur even in liberal papers, such as the weekly *Die Zeit* (The Time) or the left Berlin daily paper *Die Tageszeitung* (The Daily Newspaper). In recent years, some second-wave feminists, most prominently Alice Schwarzer, editor of *Emma*, the oldest feminist magazine in Germany, discursively joined the anti-gender forces by criticizing the supposed cultural relativism of gender theorists that allegedly legitimizes not only sexism in Muslim cultures but also Islamic terror (Schwarzer 2017).

"Gender ideology" or "gender theory"—in combination with an often violent, anti-Muslim racism—are *the* common enemy figures that unite this alliance. As we have seen with Gabriele Kuby, a common and widely used tactic is the evocation of hyperbolic and fear-arousing consequences, such as the end of "civilization-as-we know-it" if the "gender ideologues" succeed. Increasingly they also invoke us / them dichotomies, such as "we-the-people" versus the "elites," which most often means "we-the-people" versus the "gender-lobby in Brussels," or gender studies professors at German universities and abroad. What exactly "gender ideology" means is deliberately never clearly defined. Hence it functions as a free-floating signifier that can be shaped in radically different, opportunistic ways. "Gender" comes to stand for everything and anything, from destroying masculinity and femininity to requiring a ban on heterosexuality. It is also made to stand for the endorsement of LGBTIQ* rights—from marriage equality and sex education to reproductive and adoption rights—as well as for pro-choice arguments.

Gender is therefore presented as a totalitarian project of social engineering similar to other totalitarian projects, such as communism or fascism. In contrast, "anti-genderism" serves a threefold function: (1) The forces gathered under this umbrella can present themselves as the saviors of ordinary men and women, of Western civilization, and, finally, of mankind. (2) "Anti-genderism" provides the unifying ideological platform for an otherwise quite heterogeneous spectrum of neoreactionary forces (Hark and Villa 2015; 2020). (3) It serves as a cover-up for a much bigger attempt not only to change the values underlying European liberal democracies but also to reinforce racist demarcations between the West and the Rest, to use Stuart Hall's famous phrase (Hall 1992). As such, "antigenderism" is not just a feminist or gender issue but a threat to liberal democracy itself; a Trojan horse carrying forces determined to end democracy "as we know it." This is surely not the revolution some of us might have hoped for.

If this is the diagnosis, the question remains: Why gender? Why is gender able to serve as the unifying ideological platform for the authoritarian, ethnonationalist, chauvinist, maybe even protofascist project?[3] My argument here is twofold: First, gender has become a privileged battlefield for right-wing forces because it did indeed stir "trouble" as Judith Butler predicted thirty years ago. The right-wing ideologues have in fact understood that gender is a destabilizing, postessentialist concept in the sense that it questions the naturalness of *sex*. And, second, precisely because Kuby, the pope, and their comrades in spirit have understood that "gender" indeed stands for reflexivity, contingency, mobility, and the idea that things do not have to stay as they are, they transform the concept of gender into an emblem of what people fear (globalization, the loss of jobs, houses, decent income, pensions, status, security) and instrumentalize gender as a signifier of how we are all governed.[4] That is, they picture it as something that is imposed on us from above and opposes common sense, gender norms, laws of nature, biology, divine creation, and order.

If it were not so depressing, I would be tempted to say that the Right successfully appropriates Foucault's idea of resisting governance by reconfiguring gender as the emblem of imagined dark powers—of globalization, of the cosmopolitans and elites who ruin their lives, of the weird gender-bending practices of urbanites—and by instigating a political rebellion against these dark gender forces. As Wendy Brown would argue, they have succeeded in fusing freedom, rebellion, and authoritarianism seemingly without contradiction (Brown 2019). It is exactly this that we need to understand, namely how freedom—the freedom of not being subjected to "gender ideology" in this case—has become the calling card and the energy of a manifestly nonemancipatory movement. This movement heralds "illiberal democracy" in its attacks on equal rights, civil liberties, constitutionalism, and basic norms of tolerance and inclusion, and in its affirmations of white nationalism and authoritarian leadership.

It is thus no coincidence that the mobilization of us / them dichotomies between "the people" and "the establishment" are essentially played out on the field of gender and sexuality, when, for example, Gabriele Kuby argues that the Brussels gender-diktat is in fact a project of totalitarian re-education in order to produce the "sexualized gender person." Moreover, it is no coincidence that these forces coined the term "genderism" in analogy to "communism," "fascism," "totalitarianism," and "Islamism," to suggest that "gender theory" threatens the very foundations of our societies. Hence, virtually any document from any context—be it religious, academic, from organized party politics or from individual blogs or mainstream media—either explicitly states or implicitly assumes that gender studies strives for supremacy. The argument that the very notion of gender necessarily leads to or reflects totalitarianism—and will ultimately destroy our societies—is even expressed by fellow academics. As Professor Hans-Peter Klein from Johann Wolfgang Goethe University in Frankfurt/Main claims, "Gender studies overstretch their self-concept as multidisciplinary into a semi theological pretension. Accordingly, all other academic disciplines, especially those relevant for high school teachers, are expected to incorporate and teach gender studies" (Klein 2015).

If we wish to understand why it is possible to stimulate this kind of resentment against gender, we certainly have to acknowledge that feminism has in fact become part and parcel of how we are governed. At least since 1995, when the Fourth World Conference on Women was held in Beijing, women's movements around the world have sought to align themselves with the state in order to push for women's rights. While the alliance between feminism and the state certainly merits critical reflection, it is true that on many issues there is just no alternative to this alliance. Nevertheless, we must recognize that this alliance between feminism and state also stirs discomfort, resistance, and even resentment among the "ordinary people." These affects can and will be exploited and reinforced by neoauthoritarian forces.

Hence it is not just an ideological trope when, say, writers from the German right-wing paper *Junge Freiheit* (Young Freedom) complain that "Brussels is telling us how to live our relationships and how to raise our kids and so on" (Lattas 2006). This is in fact true. New legal norms *have* been enacted, and rightly so. Parents *aren't* allowed to hit their children, women *do* have equal rights, marital rape *is* punishable, lesbian and gay partnerships *are* equal before the law, to name only a few of the most fundamental achievements. These achievements can be used to incite not only political opposition but revenge, resentment, and hate. The Right has realized that because gender and sexuality hit close to home, they intensify political antagonisms to great effect.

Everyone can speak to what men and women are, and no one can tell us to think differently—not bureaucrats in Brussels, not university professors, and not social studies teachers who bring queer sex education projects into the classroom.

Neoauthoritarian forces have therefore to some extent managed to reverse the meaning of the concept of gender to its opposite, namely, to a form of ideological totalitarianism that wants to force "us" all under a dictate. What is more, "gender ideology" has been deployed as a metaphor for the insecurity and unfairness produced by the current neoliberal socioeconomic order, and it is turned into a resource for the construction of antidemocratic us / them dichotomies framed by racism. Since "gender ideology" is *their* phrase, we can understand it as a form of "discursive dispossession," to use an expression coined by the German feminist sociologist Ursula Müller (1998). It is vital for us to understand the ways in which these operations of discursive dispossession work. For the paradox that gender, which stands for reflexive contingency like few other concepts, can be used to set up an emotionally charged and increasingly racist opposition between "the people" and "the establishment" seems symptomatic of dynamics that extend far beyond the field of *gender* in the political and social arena.

To understand how profound this discourse of dispossession is, I want to very briefly remind us of the history of the sociological concept of gender. For this is a critical history. It was none other than the sociologist Erving Goffman who famously declared gender as the prototype of a social category and classification. Goffman writes, "In all societies, initial sex-class placement stands at the beginning of a sustained sorting process whereby members of the two classes are subject to differential socialization" (1977, 303). Goffman explains, "It is not . . . the social consequences of innate sex differences that must be explained, but the way in which these differences were (and are) put forward as a warrant for our social arrangements, and, most important of all, the way in which the institutional workings of society ensured that this accounting would seem sound. Thus, gender here is no longer nothing more, but also nothing less, than a social classification, a defining frame, in which practice is put into effect" (1977, 302). Goffman's theory of gender resonates with the ideas of gender historian Joan W. Scott. As early as 1988 Scott argued that gender is about "perceived differences between the sexes" that are based on knowledge (1988, 42). Gender "is the knowledge that establishes meanings for bodily differences," she famously wrote in *Gender and the Politics of History* (1988, 2). If *sexual difference* can only be seen in the body as a function of our knowledge, it cannot be the causal basis from which the social order can be derived. There is, in other words, no direct path, and certainly no unilateral path, from *sex*, that is, what we commonly call biological or anatomical sex, to *gender*. Rather, it is precisely the other way around: sex has always been gender, as Butler in her famous and much-discussed thesis in *Gender Trouble* so ingeniously points out. This is nothing other than a more elaborate version of Simone de Beauvoir's 1949 assertion that we are not born but become woman.

The self-named "Anti Gender Alliance" now not only turns Beauvoir's claim upside down but effectively mobilizes against "gender ideology," which, they argue, aims to rob society of its natural founding principles: the gender binary and heterosexuality. This has led to numerous efforts to defame and discredit both scholars of gender and gender studies programs. In Germany, they accuse gender studies of being "excessive," an "ideology," a "pseudo-religious dogma," or "pseudo-science." They argue that gender studies is out of touch with reality and that the field ignores both scientifically proven and objective facts and "healthy human understandings."

This hostility on the part of the Far-Right Anti Gender Alliance goes hand in hand with a newly revived antistate populism. And this, in turn, is accompanied on the one hand by the mobilization of resentment about being governed at all (i.e., against an allegedly top-down indoctrination— either from the EU bureaucracy in Brussels, the state, or even gender studies professors) and on the other hand with the demand that gender studies be "socially beneficial," and comprehensible for all taxpayers in terms of both content and method. Again and again it presents an identical set of assertions, which all share the premise that gender studies is ideology not science.

The Anti Gender Alliance argues that gender studies is disproportionately influential at universities and colleges. It gives the impression that millions, even billions, of public resources are flowing into a political ideology that not only is disguised as science but, in addition, is trying to indoctrinate young people at universities. The argument that gender studies is part of raison d'état is perhaps the most important element of the discrediting rhetoric of the Right. It can be linked in many ways to populist arguments and antistate rhetoric common both in libertarian conservative and right-wing contexts. The Anti Gender Alliance couples this critique with nationalist and anti-European attitudes, often using the code word "Brussels."

It is important to note that these attacks differ from those historically made against feminism. Today the Right does not argue that women cannot have equal rights because they are inherently different. They maintain instead that women *are* inherently and fundamentally different in nature *and* deserve equal rights. Today's mobilization is organized against an academic concept, gender, and not against feminism in general.

In addition, feminism is rearticulated in right-wing discourse. It is essentially founded on naturalistic, familial, and religious—which usually means Christian—principles. This new feminism is then positioned to oppose gender, gender feminism, or "queer-feminism." The Right claims that this new feminism is closer to common sense, to the daily practices and experiences of women and men than "gender ideology," which they denounce for setting the rules, and for being conceived in Berkeley, implemented in Brussels, and taught at German colleges and universities.

This is precisely where the neoreactionary feminism of figures such as Gabriele Kuby in Germany or Marine Le Pen in France fit in. It is of utmost significance that they present themselves as feminists. In order to be able to make the claim that they are the defenders of liberty and equal rights they disavow the claim that women cannot have equal rights because they are by nature different, and, also to argue that women and men do have equal rights and yet by nature are fundamentally, essentially, clearly different ontologically.

Let me come to a conclusion. As I hope I have demonstrated, gender is the new watershed. Attacks are directed against anyone who characterizes gender and sexual desire as socially constituted, historically conditioned, culturally contingent, and grounded in practice. The antigenderist position, for its part, maintains a simplistic, epistemologically untenable, and empirically debunked naturalism in the matter of gender and sexuality. Inasmuch as they recognize the historical achievements of feminism, they regard it as a victorious movement for women's equality, beyond which the claims associated with the "gender delusion" (as they call it) become intolerable and nonsensical.

Gender is apt to unsettle and offend everyday worldly certainties. It is necessary to take the antigenderist attacks seriously *as a response* to this unsettling. But gender also brings into the light of politics and culture a whole host of previously invisible, outlawed, and marginalized experiences, norms, and modes of existence: lives beyond the gender binary, fluid sexualities, nonbinary physical and affective embodiments of sex. All of this, of course, leads to "gender trouble," which an open and democratic society ought to deal with reflexively and, of course, critically. But the bellicose, hateful, often ad hominem mudslinging to which gender studies in Germany has been subjected for over a decade is not that.

Moreover, gender is used by neoreactionary forces to disturb and confuse, and to orchestrate a new antagonism, a new us / them opposition: "the people 'against' the establishment." Far more than the reputation of gender studies is at stake. For the attacks do not aim just to harm academics and their academic work, to discredit the interdisciplinary field of gender research and denounce it as ideology. Also at stake is the explicit discrediting of science and the university as a place where reality is questioned and negotiated unconditionally, as a part of an open, democratic society that can view things from many different perspectives. The open, democratic society is itself at stake.

Finally, antigenderism is not only an element of an authoritarian, neoreactionary worldview that aims to undermine democracy as such. Rather, gender here is being mobilized in a very specific way to justify racist or anti-Islamic policies of exclusion. All over Europe today we are witnessing xenophobic, nationalistic parties, but also neoliberal regimes, increasingly using concepts of equal rights to claim that male Muslim citizens—and non-Western male migrants in general—are not capable of respecting the rights of *women* and LGBTIQ* people. Neofascist parties claim to support women's rights while denouncing Islam to generate more overt hatred and hostility, and thereby incite violence toward migrant communities and nonwhite people. Marine Le Pen, for example, appeared in the last French presidential election campaign as a kind of women's rights campaigner, targeting precisely those women who believe the *Front National* is a bulwark against immigration and a Europe of open borders, both detrimental to women's rights and liberties. Le Pen managed to portray herself as a person who advocates on behalf of the separation of religion and state against an aggressive Islam that fights precisely against *laïcité* or secularism.

The "enlightened fundamentalism" to use a term coined by political scientist Liz Fekete (2006), of right-wing populism in Europe is revealed not only by how women, lesbians and gays, and other minorities are instrumentalized for xenophobic politics, but also by a certain aggressive attitude, which shapes toxic speech. In regard to feminism, this combativeness is to a certain extent double-edged and contradictory. On the one hand, right-wingers claim feminism for their own purposes to agitate against migration, Islam, and foreigners. On the other, they use it to demonize feminists who question hegemonic gender and sexuality norms. They therefore fight inwardly against the so-called genderistas and queers, who supposedly impose on ordinary people, whom they picture as uncivilized, inferior others, their ideas of how sex and sexuality should be lived.

The tendency to "other" nonwhites, non-Westerners, and non-Christians, with the intention of keeping them at a distance, is thus directly linked to the defamation of sexual and gender minorities and feminist dissenters. Political parties in Germany, such as the Alternative für Deutschland and Pegida, campaign not only against the "Islamization of the West" but also against what they themselves call its "genderization."

The way in which nationalistic and xenophobic parties and national-conservative regimes mobilize gender and sexuality is certainly one of the most significant aspects of the current political situation. The question is how we should react to these dynamics. We should not enter into a debate about what is a true or false statement in relation to gender. Nor should we subject ourselves to the framework of self-victimization created by right-wing forces. As feminist academics, we must dare to be critical when confronted by the political challenge of the neoreactionary seizure of democracy.

Notes

1. Such as the Alternative für Deutschland (AfD) in Germany, Rassemblement National (RN) in France, the Freiheitliche Partei Österreich (FPÖ) in Austria, the Partij voor de Vrijheid in The Netherlands, PiS (Law and Justice) in Poland, Fidesz, the Party of Victor Orban in Hungary, and Jair Bolsonaro's Partido Social Liberal in Brazil.
2. See also Hark and Villa 2015.
3. In a similar vein, Eszter Kováts and Maari Põim speak of "gender as symbolic glue." See Kováts and Põim 2015.
4. For an extended version of this argument see Hark and Villa 2020, 77–108.

References

Brown, Wendy. 2019. *In the Ruins of Neoliberalism: The Rise of Antidemocratic Politics in the West*. New York: Columbia University Press.

Butler, Judith. 2019. "What Threat? The Campaign against 'Gender Ideology.'" *Glocalism: Journal of Culture, Politics and Innovation* 3:1–12. doi:10.12893/gjcpi.2019.3.1.

Fekete, Liz. 2006. "Enlightened Fundamentalism? Immigration, Feminism and the Right." *Race & Class* 48 (2): 1–22.

Goffman, Erving. 1977. "The Arrangement between the Sexes." *Theory and Society* 4 (Fall): 301–331.

Hall, Stuart. 1992. "The West and the Rest: Discourse and Power." In *Formations of Modernity*, edited by Stuart Hall and Bram Gieben, 275–331. Cambridge: Polity Press.

Hark, Sabine, and Paula-Irene Villa (eds.). 2015. *Anti-Genderismus: Sexualität und Geschlecht als Schauplätze aktueller politischer Auseinandersetzungen*. Bielefeld: transcript Verlag.

———. 2020. *The Future of Difference: Beyond the Toxic Entanglement of Racism, Sexism and Feminism*. London: Verso.

Klein, Hans-Peter. 2015. "Heldenhafte Spermien und wachgeküsste Eizellen." *Frankfurter Allgemeine Zeitung*, May 30, 2015. https://www.faz.net/aktuell/politik/inland/gender-studies-gender forschung-auch-in-der-biologie-13603216.html.

Kováts, Eszter, and Maari Põim, eds. 2015. *Gender as Symbolic Glue: The Position and Role of Conservative and Far Right Parties in the Anti-gender Mobilizations in Europe*. Brussels: Foundation for European Progressive Studies and Friedrich-Ebert-Stiftung. http://www.feps-europe.eu/assets/cae464d2-f4ca-468c-a93e-5d0dad365a83/feps-gender-as-symbolic-glue-wwwpdf.pdf.

Kuby, Gabriele. 2015. *The Global Sexual Revolution: Destruction of Freedom in the Name of Freedom*. Brooklyn: Angelico Press.

———. n.d. Personal Website. Accessed September 10, 2020. https://www.gabriele-kuby.de.

Lattas, Peter. 2006. "Neue Spielwiese für Feministinnen." *Junge Freiheit* 28/06. https://jungefreiheit.de/archiv/.

Müller, Ursula. 1998. "Asymmetrische Geschlechterkultur in Organisationen und Frauenförderung als Prozeß—mit Beispielen aus Betrieben und der Universität." *Zeitschrift für Personalforschung* 2:123–142.

Osborne, Samuel. 2016. "Pope Francis Says Gender Theory Is Part of a 'Global War' on Marriage and Family." *The Independent*,

October 2, 2016. https://www.independent.co.uk/news/people
/pope-francis-catholic-church-gender-theory-global-war
-traditional-marriage-family-a7341226.html.

Presidency of the Republic of Brazil. 2019. "In Inaugural Speech,
Bolsonaro Calls for Support to Rebuild the Country." January 2019. http://www.brazil.gov.br/about-brazil/news/2019/01
/in-inaugural-speech-bolsonaro-calls-for-support-to-rebuild-the
-country.

Ratzinger, Joseph, and Angelo Amato. 2004. "Letter to the Bishops
of the Catholic Church: On the Collaboration of Men and
Women in the Church and in the World." http://www.vatican
.va/roman_curia/congregations/cfaith/documents/rc_con_cfaith
_doc_20040731_collaboration_en.html.

Schwarzer, Alice. 2017. "Der Rufmord," *Die Zeit*, August 9, 2017.
https://www.zeit.de/2017/33/gender-studies-judith-butler
-emma-rassismus.

Scott, Joan Wallach. 1988. *Gender and the Politics of History*. New
York: Columbia University Press.

3

Ascetic Masculinity
and Right-Wing Populism in
Hindu Nationalist India

AMRITA BASU

In many ways Indian prime minister Narendra Modi con-
forms to the profile of right-wing populist leaders. Like
Vladmir Putin, Recep Tayyip Erdoğan, Jair Bolsonaro,
Rodrigo Duterte, and Donald Trump, he is authoritarian,
xenophobic, and Islamophobic, and claims to personify
"the people." Yet, in one important respect, Modi differs
from most right-wing populist male leaders who conflate
strength with virility and often misogyny and homophobia. Modi's performative style is generally mild mannered,
self-effacing, and circumspect, traits that are often considered soft and feminine. He assumes the aura of a religious
renunciate while displaying muscular aggression and commitment to a sectarian nationalist agenda. How is this read
in the Indian context? To what extent does this explain
Modi's continued popularity amid low growth rates and
civic unrest in India and his success relative to other leaders

cross-nationally? These questions form the agenda of this chapter.

To illustrate the important and perhaps surprising contrasts between Modi and other right-wing populist leaders, consider a few examples.

Silvio Berlusconi, four times prime minister of Italy, boasted about having sex with eight women in a single night (Kington 2011). He was embroiled in several scandals involving sex workers and famously defended himself by boasting that it was better to be passionate about women than to be gay (Scherer 2010).

Rodrigo Duterte, president of the Philippines, linked his love of his people with his sexual prowess. He bragged about simultaneously having two wives and two girlfriends (Brizuela 2015) and insulted the American ambassador with homophobic slurs (Chan 2016).

When a female lawmaker accused him of rape, Jair Bolsonaro, Brazil's president, responded that she was not "worth raping" because she was "too ugly" (Greenwald and Fishman 2014). He has advised parents to engage in corporal punishment of boys who show signs of being gay to ensure that they will become "proper" men.

Turkish president Recep Tayyip Erdoğan has sought to outlaw abortion and urged women to have at least three, preferably five, children for the sake of the economy (Arsu 2012). He has banned LGBTQ cultural events and declared that empowering queer and transgender people in Turkey was "against the values of our nation" (Shaheen 2017).

Russian president Vladmir Putin told a BBC journalist that Israeli president Moshe Katsav was a "mighty man" for raping ten women. "He surprised us all—we all envy him" (Parfitt 2006). Putin dismissed rumors about Trump hiring Russian sex workers: "[Trump is] . . . someone who has been involved with beauty contests for many years and has met the most beautiful women in the world. I find it hard to believe that he rushed to some hotel to meet girls of loose morals, although ours are undoubtedly the best in the world" (Beauchamp 2017). He said he'd prefer not to shower next to a gay man. "Why provoke him? But you know, I'm a judo master" (Trimble 2017).

And then of course there is Donald Trump, whose speeches are replete with overt and covert references to his sexual prowess. He has condoned rape and sexual assault and valorized aggressive masculinity. He proclaimed on TV that he had big hands—and not just big hands (Krieg 2016). He has boasted about his high testosterone levels and said that he's irresistible to women and therefore entitled to force himself on them (Belluz 2016).

The sexual bravado and macho, homophobic views of right-wing populist leaders serve multiple purposes. They signal aspirations to create a gender order based on heterosexual male dominance. Through crude, abrasive remarks, these leaders identify with stereotypical male working-class worldviews, while distancing themselves from what they consider bourgeois niceties. They feminize established elites to justify humiliating, denigrating, and bullying them. Conversely, they depict historically disenfranchised racial and ethnic minorities as dangerously hypermasculine. They suggest that representative institutions are unnecessary because they can personally provide simple solutions to complex policy matters. They pose as protectors of the people from internal and external enemies. Erdoğan often refers to his supporters and the nation as "my people," implying a patriarchal connection between the head of the nation and the father as head of household. In claiming to protect "Russians against 'pedophiles' in the Sochi Olympics in 2014, Putin positions himself as the father/savior of the nation" (Eksi and Wood 2019, 740, 744).

In contrast to leaders who are vulgar, crass, sexist, and voluble, Prime Minister Modi has generally been restrained and understated. Whereas Duterte, Berlusconi, Trump, and Erdoğan boast that they are rich and brandish their wealth, Modi proudly speaks of being born into a poor, lower-caste family. Whereas most populist leaders exaggerate their power, Modi describes himself as an ethical, incorruptible, selfless ascetic. Rather than flaunt his sexual prowess, Modi describes himself as a celibate. He had an arranged marriage at the age of eighteen but left his wife a few months later and joined the Rashtriya Sawayamsevak Sangh (RSS), a Hindu nationalist organization that requires *swayamsevaks*, Hindu men over the age of eighteen who subscribe to its goals, to become celibate.

Unlike most other right-wing populist male leaders, Modi depicts himself as a proponent of women's rights and well-being. He has praised women's entrepreneurial abilities and called for women to become financially independent so that they can become stakeholders in decision making. He has asserted that "women are two steps ahead of men. We need to recognize their power" (Zeenews Bureau 2013). He has called on parents to monitor their sons to prevent sexual violence: "Have these parents ever asked their sons where they have been going, who they have been meeting? Rapists are somebody's sons as well! Parents must take the responsibility to ensure that their sons don't go in the wrong direction" (Economic Times 2014). He has criticized the use of amniocentesis for sex-selective abortions: "Have we seen our sex ratio? Who is creating this imbalance? Not God. I appeal to the doctors not to kill the girl child in the mother's womb. I request the parents not to kill daughters because they want a son. Don't kill daughters in the womb, it is a blot on 21st century India" (Ghosh 2014).

Although we sometimes mistakenly assume that populist leaders draw on a common script, populist performances are most effective when they mine—and in the process rewrite—historical myths and memories. As Cynthia Enloe playfully notes, we might locate the cultural repertoires of Trump in the New York City real estate developers' world of the 1970s, Putin in the KGB of the 1980s, and Erdoğan in the Law and Justice Party and its predecessor (Cynthia Enloe, pers. comm.). Modi's multivocal style of communication makes symbolic references that are embedded in Indian cultural and historical traditions.

Like other right-wing populist leaders, Modi appeals to the "common person," and expresses disdain for liberal, educated elites. However, these claims are made more credible because, unlike many of his global counterparts, Modi describes himself as a simple, humble man and an outsider to politics. His performance of sacrifice, service, and renunciation is tethered to his deeply held religious nationalist commitments. Compared to Trump, who is commonly recognized as using religion for instrumental political ends, Modi is considered a deeply religious person. Compared to the populist leaders described earlier, Modi combines characteristics that are typically associated with both masculinity and femininity.

I argue that Modi's leadership style seeks to reconcile long-standing tensions between two radically different political traditions—of Hindu nationalists and M. K. Gandhi. Modi seeks to rewrite history by claiming for himself and for the RSS a place in the anticolonial nationalist movement. Repudiating Congress party leaders for their elitism, he positions himself as Gandhi's heir. At the same time, by selectively appropriating and renouncing Gandhi's vision, Modi poses as a modern leader who can deliver jobs, economic growth, and national security.

This chapter begins with a discussion of the literature on populist leadership. I then examine Modi's shift from a masculinist style that was openly, blatantly, militantly anti-minority to his adoption of a softer, kinder, more feminine aura. I then analyze the intellectual and cultural sources of Modi's leadership style. The most important influence is the Hindu nationalist tradition of militant asceticism exemplified by Yogi Adityanath. The final section explores the ways Modi seeks to emulate and appropriate Gandhi and render him obsolete.

Populist Leadership

The populist leader does not simply represent "the people," Benjamin Moffitt writes, but is actually thought to embody the people (Moffitt 2017). Populism should not be understood simply as a set of ideas or a way of organizing followers but as a performance in which populist leaders present themselves as strong, virile, and healthy in order to present "the people" as tough and unified. This implies that populism is a political style, a repertoire of embodied, symbolically mediated performances that navigate the political, broadly defined, from the domain of governance to everyday life. These performances encompass both verbal and nonverbal forms of communication and make extensive use of the media.

Populist leaders are the central affective focus of populist followers because they perform and render present "the people." The challenge for populist leaders, Moffitt argues, is to appear both ordinary (i.e., as one of the people) and sufficiently extraordinary to rise above the people and act as their representatives (by claiming celebrity status, acting rude and disruptive, and asserting their virility). Other attributes of populist leadership include opposing pluralism, minority rights, and established elites, issuing emotional appeals, identifying with the majority, expressing disdain for representative institutions, and falsely depicting themselves as political outsiders.

If there are some commonalities, there are also significant differences in populist leadership styles across nations and genders. Most scholarship on right-wing populist leaders concerns Europe, the United States, and to some extent Latin America. One might infer from this lacuna in the scholarly literature that right-wing populism is exclusively a Western phenomenon and that the concept of populism is useful only in this context. However, the rise and prevalence of right-wing populism in the postcolonial world challenges the assumption that populism is Western and that postcolonial populism is derivative. It invites us to analyze the influences of histories of colonialism, anticolonial nationalism, and postcolonial experiences of globalization and neoliberalism. It encourages us to appreciate the inseparability of populism and nationalism in formerly colonized nations.

Scholars generally define European populism as analytically distinct from nationalism. They argue that because populism lacks strong ideological commitments, it often becomes tethered to other ideologies like nationalism (Mudde 2004, 541–563). Although a few scholars (e.g., Brubaker 2019) have argued that populism and nationalism are interdependent, since they both rest on distinguishing insiders from outsiders, I contend that the relationship between populism and nationalism is even closer in many contexts. Right-wing populism in India is ideologically robust rather than thin. Its nationalist roots hark back to the colonial past and are sustained by the postcolonial environment.

There is also a dearth of scholarship on how populism is gendered, particularly in the postcolonial world (Abi-Hassan 2017; Mudde and Kaltwasser 2014). Here again, most studies on the subject focus on Europe. Scholars have explored the strategies that right-wing populist parties adopt to attract female voters, the role of women leaders in soft-ening the image of their parties, antigender campaigns launched by right-wing populists and Christian conser-vatives, and the vilification of Muslim men as misogynist and homophobic (Erzeel and Rashkova 2017; Norocel 2011; Spierings et al. 2015). They have shown that certain European right-wing populists have supported women's rights, sometimes with the backing of white feminists, to pursue anti-immigrant agendas (Farris 2017). What remains to be theorized is the gendered character of male right-wing populist leadership.

As noted earlier, to fully understand populism we must see it not only as an ideology or organization but also as a practice or performance. Feminists have much to contrib-ute to our understanding of the gendered performances of male right-wing populist leaders since they have been at the forefront of theorizing embodiment (Butler 1986; Mahmood 2001). Whether populist leaders perform virility or celibacy, they identify their own bodies with those of the people they seek to represent.

There is a rich literature on nationalism that analyzes its double-edged implications for women and the ways bound-aries of belonging and exclusion are gendered. Some studies explore the way ethnic/racial majorities use gendered tropes to vilify men from minority communities. However, we are only beginning to theorize the meanings of manhood and masculinity over time and in varied cultural contexts and to appreciate the way they animate politics (Sinha 1999). As Tamar Mayer notes, the preoccupation of feminist scholar-ship with recovering women's voices and experiences has resulted in their devoting inadequate attention to men and the constructions of masculinity (Mayer 2000). The story of nationalism and men's work for the nation is well doc-umented; Mayer writes, "That story is true everywhere:

prowess, virility, aggressive warriors who save the nation, rivers that flow with boys' blood, young men who fight for the land and become the silver platter on which independence is attained." She goes on to say that theories of nationalism have yet to grapple with the varied shades of gender identities and tones of nationalism (Tamar Mayer, pers. comm.).

Few studies of right-wing populism in India focus on men and masculinity (some important exceptions include Banerjee 2012 and Chopra 2006). Most existing studies link Hindu nationalist violence to its hypermasculinity (Anand 2011; Banerjee 2012; Kinnvall 2019). It is true that Modi displays muscular nationalism, flaunting his imposing physical stature and comportment and boasting that he has the body of a wrestler (an allusion to the RSS wrestling tradition). His 2014 campaign speeches were peppered with references to his *chappanese chaatte* (56-inch chest). However, I contend that scholars have ignored the way Modi not only displays assertive masculinity but also prototypical soft and feminine attributes. In parallel fashion, while his performance of humility encourages Hindus to see him as subaltern, his display of physical strength implies that he can protect them from Indian Muslim minorities and from Pakistan.

Modi's Oscillating Leadership Style

Modi's leadership style has been more inconsistent than that of many other right-wing populist leaders. During the time he served as chief minister of Gujarat (2001–2014), Modi demonstrated masculine aggression. By contrast, in his bid to become prime minister in 2014, Modi depicted himself as kind, humble, and judicious. He claimed to identify with the lower classes and castes, and with women. In seeking reelection in 2019, Modi combined the aura of being simple, humble, and self-sacrificing, with commitment to a hardline

Hindu nationalist agenda. His rebranding on both occasions was extremely electorally successful. After the 2014 elections, one in four respondents who were surveyed said they voted for the Bharatiya Janata Party (BJP)-led National Democratic Alliance because Modi was the prime ministerial candidate (Chhibber and Verma 2014). In 2019, 83 percent of 2,000 respondents identified Modi as the top choice of candidate for prime minister.

Modi's leadership style as chief minister of Gujarat was the antithesis of what it is today. Under his watch, Hindu nationalist organizations perpetrated mass violence, killing over 1,000 people, mostly Muslims; Modi openly condoned their violent actions. After a train in Godhra (a municipality in Gujarat) caught fire, killing a number of Hindu nationalist activists, the RSS and its affiliates organized mass violence against Gujarati Muslims. Modi claimed that this violence was an understandable reaction to the fire. He declared, with no evidence, that either the Pakistani government or jihadis were responsible for what he described as a premeditated act of terrorism (Vardarajan 2002, 5). After the violence, while touring Gujarat during the 2002 state election campaign, Modi defended the killings in one locality by saying, "It should be remembered, they occurred because of the Godhra carnage" (Desai 2002). More often he has engaged in dog whistling, conveying controversial messages about Muslims indirectly, as the following comment he made in September 2002, in the aftermath of the violence, suggests: "What should we do? Run relief camps for them? Do we want to open baby-producing centers? We are five and they are twenty-five. Gujarat has not been able to control its growing population and poor people have not been able to get money. There's a long queue of children who fix tire punctures. In order to progress, every child in Gujarat needs education, good manners, and employment.

That is the economy we need. For this, we need to teach a lesson to those who are increasing the population at an alarming rate" (quoted in *The Tribune* 2002). Modi has yet to express regret or remorse for the 2002 violence against Muslims.

A year later, as the 2014 parliamentary elections approached, Modi and his campaign advisers worked with major media and advertising firms to refashion his image. Candidate Modi appeared to be incorruptible, humble, and inspiring. He identified with the suffering and struggles of the common people and promised them jobs, development, and growth. Modi appeared in innumerable posters, holograms, and twitter feeds not only as a powerful political leader but also as a savior and visionary. He rhetorically and bodily commanded and engaged his audiences, summoning humor, spontaneity, and carefully crafted imagery to elicit intense affective responses (Doval 2016).

Since 2014 Modi has depicted himself in populist fashion as a man of humble origins, from a poor, lower (Other Backward Class) background in part to differentiate himself from the former political establishment of the Nehru–Gandhi dynasty. Modi's repeated references to his low caste and class background also appeal to the aspirations of upwardly mobile youth (Mitra and Schöttli 2016). During the 2014 election campaign, he capitalized on a Congress Party leader's derisive description of him as a son of a tea seller by organizing a series of streamed conversations at roadside chai (tea) stalls as well as a radio series *Mann Ki Baat* (Matters of the Heart).

In one of his many speeches on this theme he proclaimed, "This is the beauty of India's Constitution, this is its capability which has made it possible that today a boy from a small town, a poor family, has the opportunity to pay homage to the tri-colour of India at the ramparts of Lal Quila

[Red Fort]" (Indian Express 2014). In a speech at New York's Madison Square Garden in September 2014, he proclaimed, "I am a small and insignificant person. My childhood, too, was insignificant. I want to concentrate on small things because I am a small person, who wants to accomplish big feats for other small people" (Mitra and Schöttli 2016).

After assuming office in 2014, Modi described himself as an outsider to political life. In a speech on the sixty-eighth anniversary of Independence Day, he declared, "Brothers and sisters, I am an outsider . . . I am not a native of Delhi. I have no idea about the administration and working of this place. I have been quite isolated from the elite class of this place but during the last two months while being an outsider, I had an insider view and I was astonished" (Modi 2016a). He repeated this theme in his interview with TV talk-show host Arnab Goswami: "I do not have any previous baggage because I've had a clean slate. I write everything from the beginning and that has a benefit. Today we are building relations with countries across the world" (Modi and Goswami 2016).

On a related theme, Modi has expressed his willingness to take risks and express unpopular views because he claims that unlike most political leaders and parties, who reduce democracy to elections, he is indifferent to power. He claimed, in an interview, that "those who have seen me in Gujarat, and those who have seen me in the last two years, those who see me without any bias, they will know that I am an apolitical prime minister. Apart from elections, I don't get involved in politics ever" (Modi and Goswami 2016). Underlying his attack on Congress Party candidate Rahul Gandhi in the 2019 election, which resulted in his reelection for another term, was Modi's identification of himself with the subaltern, and Congress with the corrupt elite. Modi described himself in this election campaign not as a *naamdar* (member of a dynasty), but as a *kamdar* (working person). He responded to Rahul Gandhi's slogan "chowkidar chor hai" (the watchman is the thief) by affirming his identity as a *chowkidar* (watchman) and launching a Twitter campaign #MainBhiChowkidar (I too am a watchman). Modi thereby turned on its head Rahul Gandhi's disparaging depiction of him as a watchman, asserted that India needed *chowkidars*, not rulers, and promised to safeguard democracy from established elites. In his first speech after winning a second term in office, he asked the electorate to hold him accountable and promised not to make personal gains from public office but to dedicate himself to serving the nation.

Traditions of Asceticism and Renunciation

Modi's culturally resonant claims to be incorruptible, humble, and an outsider to politics are rooted in a long history of political asceticism. The starting point for understanding the role of asceticism in Indian politics is colonialism and its legacies. The British considered asceticism an obstacle to India's progress and as justifying, indeed necessitating, colonial rule. They also sowed the seeds of religious tensions by claiming that Hindus had enjoyed a golden age in the past that Muslim rule had destroyed. They thereby depicted Muslims as predatory, aggressive outsiders who had rendered Hindus, India's original inhabitants, weak and effeminate.

As Ashis Nandy (1983) famously argued, British colonizers relied heavily on gendered tropes. They embraced supposedly masculine qualities associated with rationality, industriousness, and dominance; they attributed to Hindus "feminine" qualities of irrationality, slothfulness, and submissiveness. Among the many responses to colonial thought, two were especially significant: that of Hindu nationalists, who largely accepted British colonial stereotypes and viewed British domination as proof of their masculine superiority, and that of Gandhi, who rejected them. Although as Nandy argues, the Gandhian view prevailed, Hindu nationalism became its ghostly double (Wakankar 1995).

The antipathy between the RSS and Gandhi became acute in 1947, amid the Partition of the subcontinent. Gandhi's assassin, Nathuram Godse, was affiliated with the RSS and blamed Gandhi for Partition. BJP member Pragya Singh Thakur, who was elected to parliament in 2019, delivered fiery campaign speeches in which she hailed Godse as a patriot (ANI 2019). The RSS also hated Gandhi for challenging colonial stereotypes about gender and ethnicity. As Gyanendra Pandey notes, since the 1940s, militant Hindu organizations have periodically asked how Mahatma Gandhi, with his feminine *charkha* (spinning wheel), could possibly be considered the "Father of the Nation" (Pandey 1993).

Like Orientalists, the RSS attributes fixed and unchanging characteristics to Muslims, who it depicts as inherently aggressive. Although it believes that Hindus' tolerance has emasculated them, it seeks to cultivate virile masculinity through physical training and ideological indoctrination. M. S. Golwalkar (1966), who is considered the ideological guru of the RSS, argues, "The foremost task before us . . . is the moulding of . . . a self-sacrificing and disciplined and virile national manhood. And verily, this is the one mission to which the RSS is wholly and solely dedicated."

Modi's RSS training began when he was a teenager. He participated in its daily *shakhas* (training camps) in which he engaged in prayers, exercises, and ritual displays of allegiance to militarist Hindu nationalist ideals. Modi became a *pracharak* (full-time RSS volunteer) in 1967 and steadily ascended within the organization. Twenty years later, the RSS deputed Modi to the BJP and marginalized other high-ranking BJP leaders to promote his rise in Gujarat. Modi's ties to the RSS enabled him to overcome opposition to his leadership from within and outside the BJP.

Modi embodies RSS values in his performance of leadership. RSS *swayamsevaks* (volunteers) are expected to renounce family life, official titles, and monetary remuneration and dedicate themselves to national service. Modi's identification with the poor echoes the RSS commitment to disregarding caste and class distinctions and creating fraternity among Hindus. Modi's claim to be an outsider to political life, despite his having been chief minister of Gujarat from 2001 to 2014, echoes the RSS claim of being a cultural rather than a political organization, although it is firmly implanted in state bodies and civil society organizations. Modi also echoes a view, rooted in Hindu and RSS philosophy, that considers the world of politics dirty, corrupt, and unethical. The RSS expresses distrust of the political establishment, opposes representative institutions, and, until quite late in its history, opposed the formation of a Hindu nationalist political party.

In posing as a renunciate, Modi places himself within a tradition of asceticism that promotes Hindu domination and minority subjugation. Hindu nationalists' call for sacrifice and service is designed to supposedly protect the Hindu motherland from rapacious Muslims. However, over the past six years, Modi has refrained from openly provoking anti-Muslim violence. This task has fallen to the other Hindu nationalists.

One of Modi's close associates reflects all the hallmarks of militant Hindu nationalists' performance of aggressive masculinity and renunciation. Yogi Adityanath, a militant Hindu nationalist ascetic, serves as Modi's double. Whereas

Modi depicts himself as rising above the fray to humbly serve the nation, Adityanath's persona, like that of Trump, Bolsonaro, and Duterte, is loud, brash, and macho. Unlike Modi, who claims to be a humble man of the people, Adityanath is patronizing and domineering. His speeches have incited violence against women and Muslims and he has faced criminal charges for rioting, attempted murder, criminal intimidation, unlawful assembly, and endangering life or the personal safety of others. Although Adityanath has at times been disdainful of the BJP for being too moderate, he has always been a great admirer of Modi.

A comparison between Modi and Adityanath with respect to gender issues is especially striking. Modi has sought to demonstrate his commitment to women's rights by promoting a Uniform Civil Code and supporting legislation criminalizing the practice of triple *talaq* (divorce; under Shariat law, a Muslim man can legally divorce his wife by uttering or writing talaq three times). Adityanath also claims to protect Hindu women by provoking violence against Muslim men. In advance of the 2014 and 2017 elections, Adityanath alleged that Muslims were organizing an international conspiracy, a so-called love jihad (i.e., coercing Hindu women into romantic relationships, converting them to Islam, and abusing them) (Faleiro 2014; Raja 2014; Sarkar 2014). He said in a television interview that he would "not tolerate what is happening to Hindu women in the name of love jihad." He called on his supporters to convert 100 Muslim women through marriage every time a Muslim man married a Hindu (Bidwai 2015). Senior BJP leaders endorsed his views and participated in the campaign, which included trying to prevent young women from using cell phones and the Internet to avoid falling into the love jihad trap (Mahanta 2014). Modi has never condemned the love jihad campaign.

Adityanath has not only attacked Muslim men for being dangerous sexual predators but has also sought to regulate and control Hindu women's sexuality and reinforce gender hierarchies. In the love jihad campaign, Hindu nationalist activists "abduct" (or in their language, "rescue") Hindu women who are dating or married to Muslim men, and threaten them and their partners. They send them to "counseling centers," and pressure them to marry Hindu men. There are other examples of Adityanath's misogyny. In contrast to most members of the BJP, Adityanath has opposed the Women's Reservation Bill, which would provide quotas for women in the legislatures, on the grounds that it could reduce women's domestic responsibilities. He has said that if men develop feminine traits they become gods, but if women develop masculine traits they become demons (Pathak 2010).

Soon after becoming chief minister of Uttar Pradesh, Adityanath created "anti-Romeo squads," which supposedly ensure the safety of women and girls by falsely accusing men of harassing women. Most observers believe that the real purpose of these squads is to engage in moral policing of couples who choose to be together (Bhalla 2017). Modi has refused to condemn these campaigns. Although populists in the United States and Europe often attack liberal elites (recall the terms "limousine liberals" in the United States and "champagne socialists" in Britain), they do not usually police the sexuality of women from the majority community or orchestrate physical attacks on them. That this happens in India is reflective of middle-class anxieties about women's sexual freedom.

Modi and Gandhi

While remaining faithful to the RSS, Modi seeks to emulate Gandhi, despite the radical differences in their worldviews. Whereas Modi has exonerated anti-minority violence,

Gandhi abhorred violence against Muslims and undertook numerous fasts to prevent or stop it. Whereas Modi has strengthened the executive and weakened autonomous civil society associations, Gandhi opposed centralized state power and favored direct democracy. Whereas Modi embraces neoliberalism and globalization, Gandhi rejected industrialization and favored a village-based economy.

Yet in his public performance, Modi closely follows Gandhi's lead. As India's "founding father," Gandhi remains the touchstone of moral authority. Gandhi tied asceticism to religious and moral power, self-sacrifice, and national renewal (Alter 1994). By associating himself with Gandhi, Modi writes himself and the RSS into the anticolonial nationalist movement. In populist fashion, Gandhi appealed to the common person against entrenched elites and favored direct over representative democracy.

Modi also identifies himself with Gandhi to gain international acclaim. In an op-ed he wrote for the *New York Times* on Gandhi's 150th birth anniversary, Modi describes India as being a global leader in eliminating poverty and harnessing renewable resources (Modi 2019). Whereas the United States revered Gandhi, it denied Modi a visa when he was chief minister of Gujarat in 2005 because over a thousand Muslims were murdered under his watch. Modi has promoted his commitment to universal spiritual values through meditation, yoga, and Ayurveda to gain international respect. For example, he encouraged the United Nations to create an annual international yoga day on June 21 (Gupta and Copeman 2019). Home Minister Amit Shah commented that, whereas the colonizers restricted yoga to saints and seers, under Modi's leadership, India had become a *vishwa guru* (teacher to the world). These "new age" cults and gurus often have links to sectarian ideologies and organizations (Sharma 2016).

Modi speaks about the importance of changing the world's perceptions of India by challenging Orientalist stereotypes. Take, for example, his speech at Madison Square Garden in New York soon after he was first elected, in which he said, "Till only 25–30 years back, if not more, there were many people in the world who thought that India was a country of snake charmers, it was a country which practiced black magic. The real identity of India had not reached the world, but my dear brothers and sisters, our youngsters, 20-22-23 years old youngsters have mesmerized the whole world with their skills in computers. Our young I.T. professionals have given a new path of making a new identity of India" (Modi 2016b). Modi appeals to middle class Indians' sense that the West has not fully recognized India's past contributions or future potential. A consistent theme is Indian pride. Speaking to an Indian audience in Shanghai in May 2015, Modi declared, "Earlier, you felt ashamed of being born Indian. Now you feel proud to represent the country. Indians abroad had all hoped for a change in government last year" (Haider 2015). In a speech in Seoul, he suggested that Indians have ceased to be despondent and pessimistic, by implication, as a result of his leadership: "There was a time when people used to say we don't know what sins we have committed in our past life to be born in Hindustan . . . let's leave. And they left. Even businessmen didn't want to do business here. Most people then had one foot abroad. They were gripped by pessimism and rage. . . . Now, people from all walks of life want to come back to India, even if it means having a lower income. The mood has changed" (Gupta 2018). Gandhi today has become an open signifier. Vinay Lal writes, "What is palpably true, and something that calls for continued reflection, is that 'Gandhi' has become, if he has not been for some time, an empty vessel—and we will pour into it what we choose" (Lal 2007). As Faisal Devji argues,

"Gandhian politics were fully portable and replicable through bodily practices that entailed patience, stubbornness, and sacrifice. . . . The techniques of self-rule didn't rest on particular external conditions as they were situated in bodies, intimacies, and localities" (Birla and Devji 2011).

Modi has invoked Gandhi to appropriate and reinterpret him. Take, for example, one of Modi's major campaigns—to improve sanitation. The BJP's 2014 election manifesto promised a "Swacch Bharat" (Clean India) and Modi began the campaign on October 2, 2014, Gandhi's birthday (known in India as Gandhi Jayanti). He launched the campaign with a symbolically significant gesture: sweeping the streets of Delhi with a broom. In his speech that day he said that there was no better way to honor Gandhi's 150th birth anniversary in 2019 than by cleaning up India because Gandhi valued cleanliness above all else. Although Gandhi was notoriously concerned with cleanliness, to say he prioritized cleanliness over freedom extricates one of Gandhi's goals from his broader social platform (Palshikar 2014).

On Gandhi's birthday in October 2017, Modi stated, "Mahatma Gandhi is as relevant to the world now as he was during his lifetime. . . . For Mahatma Gandhi, cleanliness was more important than freedom. . . . Let us all walk on the footpath laid down by Mahatma Gandhi and fulfill his wishes" (Indian Express 2017). To oversee the Swacch Bharat campaign, Modi established a committee that included several foreign dignitaries. India also hosted a Mahatma Gandhi International Sanitation Convention in 2018 to share best practices around sanitation.

Modi's Swacch Bharat campaign was symbolically significant. Cleaning the streets could be a metaphor for cleaning up public life—ending corruption. Cleanliness has connotations of purity and respectability for racist right-wing groups. Picking up a broom and cleaning the streets also identifies Modi with poor, lower-caste street cleaners and women who clean the home. Another government scheme that is designed to appeal to women, "No Toilet, No Bride," makes the creation of private toilets a requirement for registering marriages and receiving financial benefits.

At the same time, a clean start signals a new beginning, a new dawn of independence. India's colonial rulers regarded the public performance of bodily functions as a mark of India's primitive failure to distinguish between public and private domains (Doron and Rajan 2015). Earlier generations of nationalist leaders sought to improve sanitation and public health but met with subaltern resistance to the imposition of bourgeois norms (Chakrabarty 2002). Modi's sanitation schemes signify that India will make itself more presentable to the Indian middle classes and the West.

In keeping with RSS tenets, Modi implies that India has not achieved complete independence because it did not liberate itself from the supposed yoke of Muslim domination. For example, in his first postelection speech in India's lower house of parliament in 2014, Modi railed against the "1,200 years of slave mentality" afflicting India: a reference not only to the 200 years of British rule, but the 1,000 years of Muslim rule that predated it (Ghose 2014).

Modi has not simply claimed an affinity with Gandhi, he has sought to elevate himself above Gandhi. For example, he took the controversial step of removing an iconic image that appears in an official calendar of Gandhi spinning and replaced it with a picture of himself at the spinning wheel. In this move, which the staff at the Khadi and Village Industries Commission protested, Modi identified himself with an important symbol of the anticolonial struggle. For Gandhi, spinning, and by extension *swadeshi* (self-sufficiency), promoted several goals, including commitment to self-reliance, self-rule, and national freedom. Given Modi's commitment to neoliberalism and globalization, his understanding of *swadeshi* is, by comparison, much thinner.

Modi also appropriates and distorts Gandhi's view of democracy. In a speech to the upper house of parliament in February 2018, he stated that Gandhi wanted a Congress-*mukht* Bharat (or a Congress-free India) after Independence. However, Modi failed to note that Gandhi's underlying motivation was to challenge the centralization of power in parties and the state, and to make Congress a people's organization.

Whereas Gandhi embraced multiple faiths and vernacular traditions, Modi purposefully and exclusively promotes Hindi. Buttressed by his training in the RSS, Modi's Hindi is expunged of Urdu words and filled with Sanskrit phrases. Although he speaks fluent English and English is one of India's two national languages, Modi generally addresses foreign dignitaries through an interpreter in Hindi. By speaking in Hindi rather than English, Modi signals his refusal to submit to the ways of Westernized, English-speaking elites. He has lashed out at "VIP culture" (Schmall 2019) and the "Khan Market gang," namely liberal, Westernized elites in a posh, cosmopolitan Delhi neighborhood (Bhardwaj 2019). Modi thereby addresses and accentuates lower middle-class resentments towards the English educated, Westernized upper middle classes. If one segment of society, the English-speaking educated elite, embrace cultural globalization, the lower-middle classes, who constitute the BJP's traditional base, fear that Westernization will undermine traditional values and family life.

Modi embodies leadership traits that seek to reconcile the tensions between asceticism and materialism. On the one hand, he calls attention to his disciplined, austere lifestyle. He is a vegetarian and a teetotaler. He boasts of awakening at five a.m. and working eighteen hours a day, taking breaks only for meditation and yoga. His self-discipline and hard work are designed to communicate his selfless devotion to the nation. On the other hand, Modi has cultivated a distinctive and expensive fashion style. He uses luxury-brand goods, such as Bvglari glasses, Movado watches, and Mont Blanc pens. He famously spent over $14,000 of public funds for a suit monogramed with his name during President Obama's visit to India in 2015. He depicts himself as a devout Hindu who upholds traditional values but also seeks the acclamation and investment of the West and of Indian elites. Shiv Visvanath writes:

> Modi realized that ascetic white was an archaic language. His PROs forged a more colourful Modi, a Brand Modi more cheerful in blue and peach, more ethnic in gorgeous red turbans. His ethnic clothes serve as diacritical markers of respect. He plays the chief in full regalia. Having earned traditional respect, he needed a more formal attire—suits for Davos, a bandhgala for national forums. Hair transplants and Ayurvedic advice served to grow his hair. Photographs show him even trying a Texan hat. Hoarding after hoarding proclaims not only the same message but a diverse attire of designer wardrobes. He senses he has to sustain himself as both icon and image of a different era. (Visvanathan 2013)

The most significant way in which Modi has appropriated and distorted Gandhi is by weaponizing religion. While Gandhi was a deeply religious person, and promoted Hinduism in public life, he affirmed the equality of all faiths. Since becoming prime minister, Modi's speeches and his symbolic gestures are suffused with Hindu appeals. When he entered parliament for the first time after his election in

May 2014, he touched his forehead on the steps, in the manner of a devotee in a house of worship and described it as a temple of democracy. In Modi's first speech in parliament, after senior BJP leader L. K. Advani said that Modi had done the BJP a "favor" by ensuring its electoral victory, Modi responded with tears in his eyes: "Can a son ever do his mother kripa (a favor)? It can never be. Like India is my mother, the same way the BJP is also my mother. And therefore, a son can never do kripa, he can only dedicatedly serve his mother. Kripa is by the party, it has done me the favour of giving me an opportunity to serve it" (Modi 2016b). In this speech Modi evokes mother three times—his own biological mother, India as a mother goddess, and the BJP as his mother. In keeping with Hindu references, Modi often ends his speeches with Bharat Mata Ki Jai (Long Live Mother India) and Vande Mataram! (I Praise Thee, Mother).

Modi's appeals to populism and religious nationalism have deepened since 2019. He claimed in his election campaign that year that unlike Congress, he was committed to defending national security and to serving all Indians rather than appeasing Muslims to gain their votes. In contrast to the 2014 election campaign, in which Modi emphasized economic issues, his 2019 campaign was xenophobic and anti-minority. He claimed that Rahul Gandhi was fleeing Hindu voters in the north by running for parliament in the southern state of Kerala, where "the majority is a minority" (Dutt 2019).

The government's decision to launch air strikes on Pakistan in response to a terrorist attack that killed Indian soldiers in Jammu and Kashmir in February 2019 played a major role in Modi's increased popularity and the BJP's reelection. Content analyses comparing Modi speeches in 2014 and 2019 find that references to Pakistan and terrorism increasingly featured in Modi's speeches (Rampal 2019). Modi called on the electorate to dedicate its votes to the military personnel who led the attack on Pakistan. Yogi Adityanath's description of the military as Modi's *sena* (army) was censured by the Indian Election Commission (Pandey 2019).

Modi cloaked his muscular, masculinist stance on terrorism and national security in the garb of religious sanctity. He contested the 2019 elections from Varanasi, one of the holiest Hindu cities. He concluded his campaign by donning saffron robes and meditating in a cave. In his first speech after the election, he applauded voters for filling his *fakir's jholi* (ascetic's bag), depicted himself as a Hindu ascetic, and enunciated principles drawn from the Hindu religious text, the Bhagavad Gita. Referencing the Mahabharata epic, Modi described the electorate as manifestations of the Hindu god Krishna:

> After the battle Mahabharata was concluded, then Sri Krishna was asked who he supported. I believe that during the time of Mahabharata, the answer Lord Krishna gave, that today in the 21st century, in the 2019 elections, 130 crore [1,300 million] population of the country has answered in the form of Lord Krishna. Krishna has answered that he was not in favour of anyone. He said that he only in favour of Hastinapur, for Hastinapur. Today, 130 crore people were standing for the country in the form of Krishna. This feeling among the people of India is the guarantee of the bright future of India. (Chakraborty 2019)

Modi alludes in this speech to a conversation between prince Arjun and his charioteer Lord Krishna in the Mahabharata. When Arjun hesitates about going to war against his own family, Lord Krishna encourages him to become a *karmayogi*, a spiritual person who is guided by duty and does not seek rewards for his work. In this passage, Modi implicitly draws a parallel between winning the elections and winning a war. In his second term as prime minister, Modi has framed anti-Muslim policies as connoting respect for Hindus (i.e., the construction of a temple in Ayodhya) or as matters of national security (i.e., the abrogation of the Constitution on Kashmir's status and amended citizenship laws).

Playing the role of the renunciate enables Modi to ostensibly stand above the fray of the dirty world of politics. He consistently delegates to others the tasks of implementing unpopular policies. He relied on chief ministers to execute the coronavirus lockdown in their states, the police to repress political dissidents, and militant Hindu nationalists like Yogi Adityanath to pursue anti-minority policies and actions. By claiming to be disengaged, Modi not only shields himself from blame when his policies fail, but also encourages people to take responsibility for government policies. For example, although most observers predicted that the BJP would suffer an electoral setback in the 2017 Uttar Pradesh elections because of the hardship caused by the government's demonetization policies, it actually made a massive electoral comeback because people responded to Modi's call to sacrifice for the national good. Nor has Modi's credibility suffered from his controversial actions in Kashmir or in altering citizenship laws.

Conclusion

A skeptic might ask, "Why take Modi's claims of asceticism and renunciation seriously? It is just a performance, a media fabrication, that belies Modi's underlying motivations and actions." I agree with my imagined interlocutor that Modi's leadership style, aided—although I would contend not wholly created—by the media, is a performance. Populism is in part a performance in which the populist leader engages in communicative strategies that are designed to inspire, alarm, arouse, and mobilize "the people." What makes this performance effective, I contend, is Modi's ability to frame it in positive religious and nationalist terms.

The synergistic relationship between religion and nationalism in the colonial and postcolonialism eras may appear to be unique to India. However, the relationship between religious asceticism and nationalism is far reaching. To cite just a few examples, traditions of religious asceticism have played an important role in Buddhist nationalism in Sri Lanka, Thailand, and Myanmar, and Islamic nationalism in Turkey, Iran, and Pakistan.

Modi's effective performance of leadership also rests on his ability to display varied gendered attributes. Innumerable reports on right-wing populist male leaders imply that their macho, muscular leadership style is key to their success. However, if strong-arm tactics enable these leaders to achieve power, it confines them to a narrow social base and often prevents them from being reelected to a second term of office. These leaders cannot draw from Modi's culturally and historically inscribed playbook. Modi's skill, I contend, lies in successfully appealing to attributes that are associated with both prototypical masculinity and femininity. He invites Indians to identify with him both through his masculinist display of power and through his feminine display of simplicity, unpretentiousness, and empathy for the quotidian indignities people suffer.

Modi's performance of humility, judiciousness, and even saintliness initially played well to Western audiences. The international press described him in glowing terms as a dignified statesman and proud nationalist when he was first elected prime minister in 2014; it has since become more critical. This performance also played well to poor, lower-caste Hindus in India. Modi was not only reelected to a second term in office by a larger margin than when he was first elected, but his popularity increased between 2014 and 2019 despite poor economic indicators, persistent unemployment, and a marked growth in politically motivated hate crimes (Safi 2019). More women voted for Modi in 2019 than in 2014. A third of all people who voted for the BJP in 2019 did so to express support for Modi rather than for the BJP or local candidates.

Even more striking is how popular Modi remained during the pandemic, particularly in comparison to Trump, Putin, and other global leaders who either belittled its seriousness or responded to it with strong-arm tactics. Despite an economic slowdown and mismanagement, government-sponsored police brutality against Muslims and political dissidents, the suffering of migrant workers who poured out of Indian cities, and tensions with China, a poll showed that 93.5 percent believe Modi was handling the virus effectively (Gettleman and Yasir 2020). One likely explanation for this is that a majority of Indians support Modi's performative leadership style. It is much easier to challenge leaders who are brash, crude, and misogynist than those who perform humility, simplicity, and selflessness and communicate through subtle symbolic acts, linguistic choices, and selective silences.

Acknowledgments

I am grateful to Arlene Stein and Sarah Tobias for inviting me to present an earlier version of this chapter at Rutgers University and for their helpful editorial advice on this chapter. Martha Ackelsberg, Cynthia Enloe, Mary Katzenstein, Mark Kesselman, Tamar Mayer, and Uday Mehta provided valuable comments.

References

Abi-Hassan, Sahar. 2017. "Populism and Gender." In *The Oxford Handbook of Populism*, edited by Cristóbal Rovira Kaltwasser, Paul Taggart, Paulina Ochoa Espejo, and Pierre Ostiguy. Oxford: Oxford University Press.

Alter, Joseph. 1994. "Celibacy, Sexuality, and the Transformation of Gender into Nationalism in North India." *Journal of Asian Studies* 53 (February): 45–63.

Anand, Dibyesh. 2011. *Hindu Nationalism in India and the Politics of Fear*. New York: Palgrave Macmillan.

Arsu, Sebnem. 2012. "Premier of Turkey Seeks Limits on Abortions." *New York Times*, May 30, 2012. https://www.nytimes.com/2012/05/30/world/europe/turkish-premier-calls-for-more-abortion-restrictions.html.

Asian News International (ANI). 2019. "#WATCH BJP Bhopal Lok Sabha Candidate Pragya Singh Thakur Says 'Nathuram Godse Was a 'Deshbhakt,' Is a 'Deshbhakt' and Will Remain a 'Deshbhakt.'" Twitter, May 16, 2019, 5.02 a.m. https://twitter.com/ANI/status/1128948842542579713.

Banerjee, Sikata. 2012. *Make Me a Man! Masculinity, Hinduism, and Nationalism in India*. Albany: SUNY Press.

Beauchamp, Zack. 2017. "Vladimir Putin Thinks Russian Prostitutes Are 'Undoubtedly the Best in the World.'" Vox, January 17, 2017. https://www.vox.com/world/2017/1/17/14296414/putin-trump-russian-prostitutes-yes-really.

Belluz, Julia. 2016. "Donald Trump's Appearance on Dr. Oz Was Surreal—and Disturbing." Vox, September 15, 2016. https://www.vox.com/2016/9/15/12902986/trump-dr-oz-surreal.

Bhalla, Nita. 2017. "India's 'Anti-Romeo Squads' Accused of Harassing Couples, Shaming Young Men." Reuters, April 5, 2017. https://www.reuters.com/article/us-india-women-harassment/indias-anti-romeo-squads-accused-of-harassing-couples-shaming-young-men-idUSKBN1771QR.

Bhardwaj, Mayank. 2019. "'Khan Market Gang': Modi Mocks His Elite Adversaries." Reuters, May 31, 2019. https://www.reuters.com/article/india-politics-khanmarket/khan-market-gang-modi-mocks-his-elite-adversaries-idUSKCN1T10KM.

Bidwai, Praful. 2015. "Politics of 'Love Jihad.'" *Daily Star*, March 7, 2015. https://www.thedailystar.net/politics-of-love-jihad-40364.

Birla, Ritu, and Faisal Devji. 2011. "Guest Editors' Letter: Itineraries of Self-Rule." *Public Culture* 23 (2): 265–268. https://doi.org/10.1215/08992363-1162012.

Brizuela, Maricar B. 2015. "Duterte: I Have 2 Wives and 2 Girlfriends." INQUIRER.net, December 1, 2015. https://newsinfo.inquirer.net/743793/duterte-i-have-2-wives-and-2-girlfriends.

Brubaker, Rogers. 2019. "Populism and Nationalism." *Nations and Nationalism* 26, no. 1. https://doi.org/10.1111/nana.12522.

Butler, Judith. 1986. "Sex and Gender in Simone de Beauvoir's Second Sex." *Yale French Studies* 72: 35–49. https://doi.org/10.2307/2930225.

Chakrabarty, Dipesh. 2002. "Of Garbage, Modernity and the Citizen's Gaze." In *Habitations of Modernity: Essays in the Wake of Subaltern Studies*, 65–79. Chicago: University of Chicago Press.

Chakraborty, Chandrima. 2019. "Narendra Modi's Victory Speech Delivers Visions of a Hindu Nationalist Ascetic." The Conversation, May 9, 2019. https://theconversation.com/narendra-modis-victory-speech-delivers-visions-of-a-hindu-nationalist-ascetic-117802.

Chan, Melissa. 2016. "Philippine Leader Calls US Ambassador 'Gay Son of a Whore.'" *Time*, August 10, 2016. https://time.com/4446262/philippine-president-rodrigo-duterte-calls-us-ambassador-gay-son-of-whore/.

Chhibber, Pradeep, and Rahul Verma. 2014. "The BJP's 2014 'Modi Wave': An Ideological Consolidation of the Right." *Economic and Political Weekly* 49 (39): 50–56.

Chopra, Radhika. 2006. "Muted Masculinities: Introduction to the Special Issue on Contemporary Indian Ethnographies." *Men and Masculinities* 9 (2): 127–130.

Desai, Darshan. 2002. "Dark Descent." *Outlook*, September 22, 2002. http://www.outlookindia.com/article/Dark-Descent/217313.

Doron, Assa, and Ira Raja. 2015. "The Cultural Politics of Shit: Class, Gender and Public Space in India." *Postcolonial Studies* 18 (2): 189–207. https://doi.org/10.1080/13688790.2015.1065714.

Doval, Nikita. 2016. "What Makes Narendra Modi a Good Speaker?" Livemint, June 9, 2016. https://www.livemint.com /Politics/yMfTQqQCb2nL4VYkHrbGhK/What-makes -Narendra-Modi-a-good-speaker.html.

Dutt, Barkha. 2019. "Opinion | In 2014, Modi Ran on Aspiration. In 2019, He Is Running on Fear." *Washington Post*, April 15, 2019. https://www.washingtonpost.com/opinions/2019/04/15 /modi-ran-aspiration-he-is-running-fear/.

Economic Times. 2014. "10 Top Quotes from PM Modi's Maiden Independence Day Speech." August 15, 2014. https:// economictimes.indiatimes.com/nation-world/10-top-quotes-from -pm-modis-maiden-independence-day-speech/take-responsibility -of-your-sons-modi-to-parents/slideshow/40308713.cms?from=mdr.

Eksi, Betul, and Elizabeth A. Wood. 2019. "Right-Wing Populism as Gendered Performance: Janus-Faced Masculinity in the Leadership of Vladimir Putin and Recep T. Erdogan." *Theory and Society* 48, no. 5: 733–751. https://doi.org/10.1007/s11186-019 -09363-3.

Erzeel, Silvia, and Ekaterina R. Rashkova. 2017. "Still Men's Parties? Gender and the Radical Right in Comparative Perspective." *West European Politics* 40, no. 4 (March): 812–820. https://doi.org/10 .1080/01402382.2017.1286181.

Faleiro, Sonia. 2014. "An Attack on Love." *New York Times*, October 31, 2014. https://www.nytimes.com/2014/11/02/opinion /sunday/its-not-jihad-its-just-love.html.

Farris, Sara R. 2017. *In the Name of Women's Rights*. Durham, NC: Duke University Press.

Gettleman, Jeffrey, and Samir Yasir. 2020. "Modi's Popularity Soars as India Weathers the Pandemic," *New York Times*, May 16, 2020.

https://www.nytimes.com/2020/05/16/world/asia/coronavirus-modi
-india.html.

Ghose, Debobrat. 2014. "1,200 Years of Servitude: PM Modi Offers
Food for Thought." Firstpost, June 13, 2014. https://www
.firstpost.com/politics/1200-years-of-servitude-pm-modi-offers
-food-for-thought-1567805.html.

Ghosh, Deepshikha. 2014. "One Daughter Can Serve Parents
Better Than Five Sons: PM Modi's Top 10 Quotes." NDTV
.com, August 15, 2014. https://www.ndtv.com/cheat-sheet/one
-daughter-can-serve-parents-better-than-five-sons-pm-modis
-top-10-quotes-649166.

Golwalkar, M. S. 1966. *Bunch of Thoughts*. Delhi: Sahitya Sindhu
Prakashana.

Greenwald, Glenn, and Andrew Fishman. 2014. "The Most
Misogynistic, Hateful Elected Official in the Democratic
World: Brazil's Jair Bolsonaro." *The Intercept*, December 11, 2014.
https://theintercept.com/2014/12/11/misogynistic-hateful
-elected-official-democacratic-world-brazils-jair-bolsonaro/.

Gupta, Bhuvi, and Jacob Copeman. 2019. "Awakening Hindu
Nationalism through Yoga: Swami Ramdev and the Bharat
Swabhiman Movement." *Contemporary South Asia* 27, no. 3
(March): 313–329. https://doi.org/10.1080/09584935.2019.1587386.

Gupta, Monobina. 2018. "The Most Visible Part of the India
Growth Story Has Been Modi's Increasing Ability to Laud
Himself." *The Caravan*, September 3, 2018. https://caravan
magazine.in/vantage/most-visible-india-growth-story-modi
-speeches.

Haider, Suhashini. 2015. "In Shanghai, PM Marks One Year in
Office," *The Hindu*, May 17, 2015. https://www.thehindu.com
/news/national/in-shanghai-pm-marks-one-year-in-office
/article7215030.ece.

Indian Express. 2017. "Gandhi Jayanti 2017: PM Narendra Modi
'Bows' to Bapu on Birth Anniversary." October 2, 2017. https://
indianexpress.com/article/india/gandhi-jayanti-pm-narendra

-modi-remembers-mahatma-bapu-on-birth-anniversary-october
-2-swachh-bharat-4870456/.

Indo-Asian News Service (IANS). 2020. "Narendra Modi: Over 93% Trust Modi Government Will Handle COVID-19 Crisis Well: Survey." *Times of India*, April 23, 2020. https://timesof india.indiatimes.com/india/over-93-trust-modi-govt-will -handle-covid-19-crisis-well-survey/articleshow/75312862.cms.

Kington, Tom. 2011. "Silvio Berlusconi Wiretaps Reveal Boast of Spending Night with Eight Women." *The Guardian*, September 17, 2011. https://www.theguardian.com/world/2011/sep/18 /silvio-berlusconi-wiretaps-sex-parties.

Kinnvall, Catarina. 2019. "Populism, Ontological Insecurity and Hindutva: Modi and the Masculinization of Indian Politics." *Cambridge Review of International Affairs* 32 (3): 283–302.

Krieg, Gregory. 2016. "Donald Trump Defends Size of His Penis." CNN, March 4, 2016. https://www.cnn.com/2016/03/03/politics /donald-trump-small-hands-marco-rubio/index.html.

Lal, Vinay. 2007. "Modi, the Mahatama, and Mendacity." UCLA Social Sciences MANAS, October 14, 2007. https://southasia .ucla.edu/history-politics/gandhi/modi-mahatama-mendacity/.

Mahanta, Siddhartha. 2014. "India's Fake 'Love Jihad.'" *Foreign Policy*, September 4, 2014. https://foreignpolicy.com/2014/09/04 /indias-fake-love-jihad/.

Mahmood, Saba. 2001. "Feminist Theory, Embodiment, and the Docile Agent: Some Reflections on the Egyptian Islamic Revival." *Cultural Anthropology* 16, no. 2 (May): 202–236. https://doi.org/10.1525/can.2001.16.2.202.

Mayer, Tamar. 2000. *Gender Ironies of Nationalism: Sexing the Nation*. London: Routledge.

Mitra, Subrata K., and Jivanta Schöttli. 2016. "India's 2014 General Elections." *Asian Survey* 56, no. 4 (2016): 614. https://doi.org/10 .1525/as.2016.56.4.605.

Modi, Narendra. 2014. "Full Text: Prime Minister Narendra Modi's Speech on 68th Independence Day." *Indian Express*, August 16,

2014. https://indianexpress.com/article/india/india-others/full
-text-prime-minister-narendra-modis-speech-on-68th-indepen
dence-day/.

———.2016a. "Prime Minister Narendra Modi's Independence Day
Address." *The Hindu*, April 20, 2016. https://www.thehindu.com
/news/resources/prime-minister-narendra-modis-independence
-day-address/article6338687.ece.

———. (2014) 2016b. "Text of Narendra Modi's Speech at Central
Hall of Parliament." *The Hindu*, October 18, 2016. https://www
.thehindu.com/news/national/Text-of-Narendra-Modi%E2%
80%99s-speech-at-Central-Hall-of-Parliament/article11624
655.ece.

———. 2019. "Why India and the World Need Gandhi." *New
York Times*, October 2, 2019. https://www.nytimes.com/2019/10
/02/opinion/modi-mahatma-gandhi.html.

Modi, Narendra, and Arnab Goswami. 2016. "PM Modi's Interview with Arnab Goswami: Full Transcript." *Indian Express*,
June 28, 2016. https://indianexpress.com/article/india/india
-news-india/pm-modis-interview-with-arnab-goswami-full
-transcript-2879832/.

Moffitt, Benjamin. 2017. *Global Rise of Populism: Performance,
Political Style, and Representation*. Stanford, CA: Stanford
University Press.

Mudde, Cas. 2004. "The Populist Zeitgeist." *Government and
Opposition* 39 (4): 541–563. https://doi.org/10.1111/j.1477-7053.2004
.00135.x.

Mudde, Cas, and Rovira Kaltwasser. 2014. "Populism and Political
Leadership." In *The Oxford Handbook of Political Leadership*,
edited by R. A. W. Rhodes and Paul Hart, 376–388. Oxford:
Oxford University Press.

Nandy, Ashis. 1983. *The Intimate Enemy: Loss and Recovery of Self
under Colonialism*. Delhi: Oxford University Press.

Norocel, Ov Cristian. 2011. "Heteronormative Constructions of
Romanianness: A Genealogy of Gendered Metaphors in

Romanian Radical-Right Populism 2000–2009." *Debatte: Journal of Contemporary Central and Eastern Europe* 19, no. 1–2 (November): 453–470. https://doi.org/10.1080/0965156x.2011.626121.

Palshikar, Suhas. 2014. "Cleansing Gandhi of Radicalism." *Indian Express*, October 6, 2014. https://indianexpress.com/article/opinion/columns/cleansing-gandhi-of-radicalism/.

Pandey, Gyanendra. 1993. *Hindus and Others: The Question of Identity in India Today*. New Delhi: Viking, 264.

Pandey, Tanushree. 2019. "EC Serves Notice to Yogi Adityanath over Indian Army Is Modi Ki Sena Comment." *India Today*, April 3, 2019. https://www.indiatoday.in/elections/lok-sabha-2019/story/election-commission-notice-yogi-adityanath-modi-ki-sena-comment-1493477-2019-04-03.

Parfitt, Tom. 2006. "Russia: Putin Praises Sexual Prowess of Israeli President." *The Guardian*, October 20, 2006. https://www.theguardian.com/world/2006/oct/20/russia.tomparfitt.

Pathak, Vikas. 2010. "Adityanath Adds to BJP Woes on Women's Bill." *Hindustan Times*, April 12, 2010. https://www.hindustantimes.com/delhi/adityanath-adds-to-bjp-woes-on-women-s-bill/story-yCKaEissuZr8PX6f1kZxHP.html.

Raja, Aditi. 2014. "VHP Steps Up Campaign against 'Love Jihad.'" *Indian Express*, September 19, 2014. https://indianexpress.com/article/india/india-others/vhp-steps-up-campaign-against-love-jihad/.

Rampal, Nikhil. 2019. "How PM Modi's Speeches Have Shifted Focus." *India Today*, April 29, 2019. https://www.indiatoday.in/elections/lok-sabha-2019/story/narendra-modi-speeches-lok-sabha-elections-1512995-2019-04-29.

Safi, Michael. 2019. "India Election Results 2019: Modi Claims Landslide Victory." *The Guardian*, May 23, 2019. https://www.theguardian.com/world/2019/may/23/india-election-results-narendra-modi-bjp-victory.

Sarkar, Tanika. 2014. "Love, Control and Punishment." *Indian Express*, October 16, 2014. https://indianexpress.com/article/opinion/columns/love-control-and-punishment/.

Scherer, Steve. 2010. "Berlusconi Says It's Better to Like Pretty Women Than Gay Men." *Bloomberg News*, November 2, 2010. https://www.bloomberg.com/news/articles/2010-11-02/berlusconi-says-it-s-better-to-be-attracted-to-pretty-women-than-gay-men.

Schmall, Emily. 2019. "India's Modi Paints Image of Hindu Ascetic Called to Power." Associated Press, May 24, 2019. https://apnews.com/d551f9335136428ab1abd22ad7cb5b6c.

Shaheen, Kareem. 2017. "Turkish LGBTI Activists Condemn 'Illegal' Ban on Events in Ankara." *The Guardian*, November 20, 2017. https://www.theguardian.com/world/2017/nov/20/turkey-bans-lgbti-events-ankara-public-order.

Sharma, Jyotirmaya. 2016. "Sri Ravi Shankar and the Pathology of New Age Cults." The Wire, March 10, 2016. https://thewire.in/religion/keep-god-and-godmen-out-of-politics-and-river-beds.

Sinha, Mrinalini. 1999. "Giving Masculinity a History: Some Contributions from the Historiography of Colonial India." *Gender & History* 11, no. 3 (November): 445–460. https://doi.org/10.1111/1468-0424.00155.

Spierings, Niels, Andrej Zaslove, Liza M. Mügge, and Sarah L. De Lange. 2015. "Gender and Populist Radical-Right Politics: An Introduction." *Patterns of Prejudice* 49 (April): 3–15. https://doi.org/10.1080/0031322x.2015.1023642.

The Tribune. 2002. "Modi's 'Anti-Minority' Speech Aired." September 15, 2002. https://www.tribuneindia.com/2002/20020916/nation.htm.

Trimble, Megan. 2017. "Putin Talks Menstrual Cycles in Stone Documentary." *U.S. News & World Report*, June 6, 2017. https://www.usnews.com/news/national-news/articles/2017-06-06/vladimir-putin-talks-menstrual-cycles-whether-hed-shower-next-to-a-gay-man-in-oliver-stone-documentary.

Vardarajan, Siddharth. 2002. *Gujarat: The Making of a Tragedy*. New Delhi: Penguin Books.

Visvanathan, Shiv. 2013. "The Remaking of Narendra Modi." *Seminar* 641 (January). https://www.india-seminar.com/2013/641/641_shiv _visvanathan.htm.

Wakankar, Milind. 1995. "Body, Crowd, Identity: Genealogy of a Hindu Nationalist Ascetics." *Social Text* 45 (Winter). https://doi .org/10.2307/466674.

Zee News Bureau. 2013. "Empower Women to Strengthen India, Says Narendra Modi." Zee News, April 8, 2013. https://zeenews .india.com/business/news/economy/empower-women-to -strengthen-india-says-narendra-modi_73725.html.

4

Hegemony as Capitalist Strategy

For a Neo-Marxian Critique of
Financialized Capitalism

NANCY FRASER

More than thirty years have passed since the 1985 publication of Ernesto Laclau and Chantal Mouffe's landmark book, *Hegemony and Socialist Strategy*. Massively influential, this book shaped the thinking of an entire generation of left-wing thinkers, setting the terms of debate for decades to come. In the Anglophone world especially, *Hegemony and Socialist Strategy* charted the path traveled by many New Leftists as they exited Marxism, substituting allegiance to "radical democracy" for "socialism" and the "new social movements" for "class struggle." Of course, the book did not itself create the conditions that favored this shift. But it perfectly captured the impulses behind it and gave them their most searching theoretical expression.[1]

Today, however, with the benefit of hindsight, we can discern a striking irony: the brilliant argumentation that guided so many leftists toward a post-Marxian worldview coincided with a major shift in the character of capitalist society, which Marxian thought might well have clarified: the shift from the state-managed capitalism of the post–World War II era to the financialized, globalizing capitalism of the twenty-first century. Overseen by central banks and global financial institutions and heavily reliant on accumulation through debt, this new regime is systematically economizing public discourse, devolving democratic decision making to "the markets," curtailing political agendas in the name of "austerity," and destroying the social worlds of billions of people.

In this context, the path to radical democracy must go through the critique of capitalism. There is no way to democratize society without confronting the force that is cannibalizing not "just" living standards, nature, and social reproduction but also the very substance of public power. Today, as never before, democratization requires structural critique and institutional transformation. And it is by no means clear that the social movements on which Laclau and Mouffe placed so much hope are up to the task. The problem is not only that these movements have failed to challenge the financialization of capitalist society—indeed, they have largely ignored it. Even worse, dominant currents within them were hegemonized by neoliberalism, recuperated to legitimate the present regime by lending it an emancipatory veneer. Tied to "progressive-neoliberal" forces throughout the world, and now a focus of "populist" ire, they are in no position to lead a counterhegemonic bloc that also includes working-class strata.

How should those of us who found inspiration in *Hegemony and Socialist Strategy* understand this situation? Does the idea of hegemonic articulation developed there afford an adequate perspective for grasping the prospects for emancipatory struggle in the current regime of financialized capitalism?

And if not, can it be fruitfully articulated with a structural-institutional critique of this regime? In other words, is it possible today to recover another Marxism, obscured in the Anglophone reception of *Hegemony and Socialist Strategy*, a Marxism that avoids the traps that book dissected, while absorbing and extending its insights?

In this chapter I address these questions in three steps. First, I outline a theoretical perspective that could in principle marry the discourse-theoretical analytic of Laclau and Mouffe with a structural-institutional critique of capitalist society. Second, I utilize the structural aspect of this perspective to sketch an account of financialized capitalism as an institutionalized social order, which harbors a *political* contradiction. Finally, I apply the discursive aspect of my perspective, which owes a lot to Laclau and Mouffe, to reflect on the grammar of present-day efforts to build an anti-neoliberal counterhegemony.

Theorizing Capitalism's Tendency to Political Crisis: Combining Institutional and Hegemonic Analysis

Famously, *Hegemony and Socialist Strategy* critiqued the orthodox Marxian tendency to "class essentialism." At least two important arguments were intertwined here: first, the argument that political subjectivation is not an epiphenomenal expression of social structure, but is constructed discursively, through processes of hegemonic articulation; and second, the argument that "class" enjoys no special a priori standing as the primary axis of struggle but is a discursively formed political identity like any other.

Both these arguments are persuasive to me, and I shall assume both of them in what follows. However, I reject the implication drawn by some readers of *Hegemony and Socialist Strategy*, and perhaps by the authors themselves, that discursive-hegemonic analysis can or should simply supplant social-structural/institutional analysis. On the contrary, I view those two approaches as complementary, not antithetical. Assuming that each by itself is incomplete and requires the other, I propose to make use of both of them here. More specifically, I propose to situate present prospects for counterhegemonic struggle in relation to social-structural and institutional features of the current order.

My claim is that prospects for emancipatory struggle today are shaped not only by the play of hegemonic articulations but also by a deep-seated structural contradiction at the heart of the capitalist society. I refer not to the economic contradiction that Marxists usually stress, but to an equally fundamental *political contradiction* that they often overlook. This contradiction can be summarized as follows: on the one hand, legitimate, efficacious public power is a condition of possibility for sustained capital accumulation; on the other hand, capitalism's drive to endless accumulation tends to destabilize the very public power on which it relies (Fraser 2014; 2015). Although it is inherent in capitalism as such, this political contradiction assumes a different form in every historically specific form of capitalist society. It has become especially acute in the *financialized neoliberal capitalism* of the present time.

To speak of the "political contradiction of financialized capitalism" is to follow Laclau and Mouffe in rejecting economism. But it is also to reject the sort of discursive idealism that some readers read in (or read into) *Hegemony and Socialist Strategy*. Thus, I reject the economistic view that reduces capitalist society to an "economic system," while also refusing its culturalist counterpart, which treats society as a discursive construction, formed of free-standing significations. For me, rather, capitalism is an institutionalized social order, whose economic subsystem depends on a set of extra-economic background conditions (Fraser 2014). These include processes of social reproduction, as scores of feminist theorists have long insisted, and a sustainable ecological order, as ecopolitical theorists have persuasively argued—but also, and most relevant here, the organizational capacities of *public power*. At several levels—state-territorial, regional, and global, public powers supply some indispensable preconditions for capital accumulation: the legal frameworks that underpin property rights, enforce contracts, and adjudicate disputes; the repressive forces that suppress rebellions, maintain order, and manage dissent; the international regimes that administer the monetary system and facilitate transborder trade; and the myriad agencies that engage in efforts to forestall or manage crises. Absent such *political* preconditions, there could be no capitalist economy—no exploitation of labor, no production and sale of commodities, no sustained accumulation of surplus value.

Capitalist societies are peculiar, however, in separating the "political" from the "economic" (Wood 1981). Whereas earlier societies merged political and economic power, capitalism has split them apart. The power to organize production is privatized and devolved to capital, which should deploy only the "natural," "nonpolitical" sanctions of hunger and need; the task of governing the remaining "noneconomic" orders, including the external conditions for accumulation, falls to the public power, which alone may utilize the "political" media of law and "legitimate" violence. In capitalism, therefore, the economic is nonpolitical, the political noneconomic.

In general, then, capitalist societies separate economy from polity, while simultaneously entrenching the dependence of the former on the latter. This peculiar relation of separation-cum-dependence is a built-in source of potential instability. On the one hand, capitalist economic production is not self-sustaining, but relies on public powers. On the other hand, its orientation to endless accumulation threatens to destabilize the very political capacities that capital needs. The effect over time, as we shall see, can be to destabilize the necessary political conditions of the capitalist economy.

Here, in effect, is a "political contradiction" inherent in the deep structure of capitalist society. Like the economic contradiction(s) that Marxists have usually stressed, this one, too, grounds a crisis tendency. In this case, however, the contradiction is not located "inside" the economy but rather at the boundary that simultaneously separates and connects economy and polity in capitalist society. Neither intra-economic nor intrapolitical, it is a contradiction *between* those two constitutive features of the capitalist social order—or rather between their respective dynamics and normative bases. Whereas economy's dynamic centers on accumulation, polity's thrust is to develop capacities for public action and stores of public support to legitimate their use. Clearly, these two orientations can conflict. Whether a conflict between them erupts openly, and if so, what form it takes, depends on how exactly the separation between economy and polity is institutionalized and on where precisely the boundaries between them are drawn. But this much at least should be clear: efforts to "liberate" economy from polity tend in the long run to be counterproductive—more likely to trigger than to circumvent capitalism's inherent tendency to political crisis.

Often, of course, capitalism's political contradiction is muted, and the associated crisis tendency remains under wraps. It becomes acute, however, when capital's drive toward boundless accumulation becomes unmoored from political control and turns against its own conditions of possibility. In that case, economy overruns polity, eating away at public power and destabilizing the very political agencies on which capital depends.

Potentially, the ramifications are twofold. One result can be an *institutional crisis*, in which public powers lack the necessary heft to govern effectively. Outgunned by private powers, such as large transnational corporations, they are blocked from making and implementing the policies needed to solve social problems. This is clearly the case today with respect to global warming and global finance. A second result can be a *crisis of hegemony*, in which public opinion turns against a dysfunctional system that fails to deliver. In that case, popular forces withdraw legitimation from existing arrangements and seek to redraw society's institutional map, in part by reinventing political powers that can serve the public interest. A hegemonic crisis of just this sort is unfolding around us today. For us, the burning question is, what is the relation between these two faces of capitalist crisis in the present conjuncture?

Hegemony and Socialist Strategy taught us that structural-institutional conditions never by themselves dictate the responses of social actors. Everything depends, rather, on the commonsense through which those conditions are experienced and interpreted. Especially consequential now, in the wake of the epochal shift from state-managed to finan-cialized capitalism, are commonsense suppositions about *distribution* and *recognition*. It is the set of received assumptions about how society should apportion jobs and income, on the one hand, and respect and membership, on the other, that shapes the responses of social actors to the present insti-tutional crisis. I shall return to this point in the third and final step of my argument.

First, however, I want to clarify this initial step. In the present section, I have outlined a way of understanding of "capitalism's inherent tendency to crisis" that differs from that of the "class-essentialist" Marxism criticized by Laclau and Mouffe. Two differences in particular are worth noting. First, far from according primacy to capitalism's tendency to *economic* crisis, I have identified a relatively autonomous and equally deep-seated tendency to *political* crisis.[2] Second, instead of assuming that "system crises" dictate the responses of social actors, I have distinguished institutional crises from crises of hegemony and problematized the relation between them. In general, then, the view of capitalist crisis presented here does not fall prey to the criticisms advanced in *Hegemony and Socialist Strategy*. There is no class essentialism here—no economism, determinism, or teleology. On the contrary, this view offers a way of combining Laclau and Mouffe's insights concerning the hegemonic aspect of capitalist society with neo-Marxian insights concerning its structural-institutional aspect and inherent tendencies to crisis.

Institutional Crisis of Financialized Capitalism: A Structural Account

So far, I have been elaborating the structure of this political crisis tendency for capitalism as such. However, capitalist society does not exist "as such," but only in historically specific forms or regimes of accumulation. The next step therefore is to historicize my account of capitalism's political contradiction in relation to its current phase.[3] Here, accordingly, I shall sketch an account of the institutional structure of financialized capitalism, which differs from that of the state-managed capitalism that preceded it. The effect will be to disclose the historically specific form in which capitalism's political contradiction appears today.

In financialized capitalism, central banks and global financial institutions have replaced states as the principal arbiters of an increasingly globalized economy. It is they, not states, who now make a major share of the rules that govern the central relations of capitalist society: between labor and capital, citizens and states, core and periphery, production and reproduction, society and nature, and—crucial for all of the above, between debtors and creditors. These last relations are central to financialized capitalism and permeate all of the others. It is largely through debt that capital now cannibalizes labor, disciplines states, transfers wealth from periphery to core, and sucks value from society and nature. As debt flows through states, regions, communities, households, and firms, it effects a dramatic shift in the relation of economy to polity.[4]

Whereas the previous regime empowered states to subordinate the short-term interests of private firms to the long-term objective of sustained accumulation, this one authorizes finance capital to discipline states and publics in the immediate interests of private investors. The effect is a double whammy. On the one hand, the state institutions that were previously (somewhat) responsive to citizens are decreasingly capable of addressing the latter's problems. On the other hand, the central banks and global financial institutions that have hobbled state capacities are "politically independent"—unaccountable to publics and free to act on behalf of investors and creditors. Meanwhile, the scale of pressing problems, most notably global warming, exceeds the reach and heft of public powers. The latter are, in any case, overmatched by transnational corporations and global financial flows, which elude control by political agencies tethered to a bounded territory. The general result is a growing incapacity of public powers to rein in private powers (Fraser 2008). Hence the proliferation in financialized capitalism of such terms as "de-democratization," "post-democracy," "façade democracy," and "zombie democracy."[5]

The new nexus of economy and polity arose in part through a transformation in the international order. We can date its beginnings to the 1970s, with the progressive dismantling of the Bretton Woods system of capital controls, fixed exchange rates, and the convertibility of the U.S. dollar to gold, which opened the floodgates of global financial speculation. Along with this went the repurposing of the World Bank and the International Monetary Fund as agents of economic liberalization. Then came new international treaties, such as NAFTA (North American Free Trade Agreement), and new "intergovernmental organizations," such as the WTO (World Trade Organization), which enshrined "free trade" and "private property" as Ur-norms able to trump domestic legislation. Orchestrated by the United States, these moves served to prolong its hegemony, despite its loss of moral authority and shift in status to a debtor nation.

The new global order helped redraw the boundaries between economy and polity at every level. In the periphery, developmental states were subjected to a fierce assault—first, in Latin America, via "the Washington Consensus," as U.S.-backed dictatorships began the process of opening markets and privatizing assets; and later, throughout the Global South, via "structural adjustment," as the International Monetary Fund and World Bank used "loan conditionalities" to compel cash-strapped postcolonial states to abandon import substitution industrialization for the shark-infested waters of the global market. Forced to scramble for hard currency, indebted states courted foreign direct investment by creating "export processing zones" and sought remittances by promoting labor emigration (Harvey 2007).

These arrangements facilitated the relocation of manufacturing to the semiperiphery, which further altered the balance of private to public power. Decimating powerful trade unions in the capitalist core, "deindustrialization" weakened support there for social democracy, while initiating a race to the bottom that has enhanced the power of capital through-out the world. Meanwhile, the abolition of capital controls deprived nearly all states of control over their currencies, put-ting them at the mercy of the bond markets and ratings agencies, and disabling previously available tools of crisis management, including the ability to "prime the pump" through deficit spending.[6] As a result, the states of the core were thrust into a position long familiar to those of the periphery: subjection to global economic forces they cannot possibly hope to control.

One response was a policy shift from "public Keynesian-ism," based on "tax and spend," to "privatized Keynesianism," which encouraged personal debt to promote continued high levels of consumer spending under otherwise unfavorable conditions of falling real wages, rising unemployment and precarity, and declining tax revenues (Crouch 2009). The effect, as we know, was the 2007–2008 financial crisis, which further solidified the hold of debt over public power. Responding to the prospect of financial meltdown, central banks and global financial institutions pressed states to bail out investors at citizens' expense, thereby provoking a rash of sovereign debt crises. Without missing a beat, these same financial institutions proceeded to compel states under assault by bond markets to institute "austerity." The effects in the Eurozone were especially catastrophic. Ignoring citizen pro-test and nullifying anti-austerity election results, the EU's governing "troika" handed over to private investors every last drop of value that could be extracted from devastated popu-lations. As a result, a European "community" once consid-ered the avatar of postnational democracy was now revealed to be the servant of finance.

Generally, financialized capitalism is the era of "gover-nance without government"—which is to say, of domination without the fig leaf of consent. In this regime, it is not states but transnational governance structures, such as the WTO, NAFTA, and TRIPS (Trade-Related Aspects of Intellectual Property Rights), which make the lion's share of the coercively enforceable rules that now govern vast swaths of social interaction throughout the world. Accountable to no one and acting overwhelmingly in the interest of capital, these bodies are "constitutionalizing" neoliberal notions of "free trade" and "private property," hardwiring them into the global regime, and thereby precluding democratically enacted laws limiting capital's freedom to abuse labor and pillage nature (Gill 1998). As neoliberal policies are constitutionalized, the political agenda is narrowed, preempted in advance.

Through a variety of means, finally, this regime has promoted the capture of public power by private (corporate) power. Examples include a rise in overt and covert lobbying; the revolving door between government and private firms; the long-term contracting out of public services to private firms, whose performance is monitored not by public political oversight but by private contract law; the rise of "public–private partnerships" oriented to serving "consumers" as opposed to citizens; and the "new public management," which enjoins public agencies to mimic the allegedly superior practices of large private firms (Crouch 2011). Through such means, and others, public power is internally colonized. Foucauldian scholars of governmentality have described this "neoliberal political rationality" very well (Dardot and Laval 2013; Brown 2015).

The overall effect has been to hollow out public power at every level. Political agendas are everywhere narrowed, both by external fiat (the demands of "the markets," "the new constitutionalism") and by internal co-optation (corporate capture, privatization, the spread of neoliberal political rationality). Matters once considered to be squarely within the purview of democratic political action are now declared off-limits and devolved to "the markets"—to the benefit of finance and corporate capital. The response to those who question these arrangements is TINA (there is no alternative). Polity must adapt to economy's laws. In the brave new world of financialized capitalism, public powers cannot deliver solutions to those in whose name they govern.

And woe unto those who object. In the current regime, capital's enablers brazenly target any public powers or political forces that might challenge them—whether by nullifying elections and referenda that reject austerity, as in Greece in 2015, or by preventing the candidacies of popular figures who appear likely to choose that path, as in Brazil in 2017–2018 and the United States in 2020. Throughout this era, too, leading capitalist interests (Big Fruit, Big Pharma, Big Energy, Big Arms, and Big Data) have continued their long-standing practice of promoting authoritarianism and repression, imperialism and war throughout the world. We owe the current refugee crisis in large part to them, as well as to the state actors to whom they are tied.

Here, then, is the institutional setting that provides the context for current political struggles. An institutional order designed to liberate economy from polity has weakened the public powers that capital needs to underwrite a sustained period of accumulation. The result is a major institutional crisis, as public powers are increasingly unable to deliver the results that capital—and the rest of us—need.[7]

Hegemonic Crisis of Financialized Capitalism: A Discourse-Theoretical Account

But that is only half the story. The flip side of an objective structural crisis is the subjective response of those living through it. In the present period, masses of people throughout the world are responding to financialized capitalism's dysfunctions by defecting from politics-as-usual. We need only mention the Brexit vote and its fallout in the UK; the election and subsequent unfolding of the presidency of Donald Trump in the United States; and the waxing fortunes of right-wing populist and quasi-fascist parties throughout the world. We should also mention, conversely, the strong showing of left-wing populist candidates in southern Europe, France, Mexico, and the United States (including some self-described "democratic-socialists") and (at one one point) of the Corbyn wing of the British Labour Party.

Different as they are, these developments suggest a widespread resolve to have done with neoliberalism and the parties that enabled it. The voters in question have rejected the reigning commonsense and the established political elites. Willing to think outside the box, they are actively seeking alternatives. The result is a new phase in the unfolding of the present crisis. The objective dysfunctions of financialized capitalism have found their subjective correlative. A "mere" conglomeration of structural impasses is now a full-blown *crisis of hegemony*. Together, these two aspects—the structural and the hegemonic—form the mutually propelling dynamics of the current conjuncture.

A two-sided crisis requires a two-sided analysis. Neither discourse analysis alone nor structural analysis alone can clarify a crisis that is at once institutional and hegemonic. Both perspectives are needed, and each must be linked to the other. The trick to is to join a structural account of financialized capitalism's contradictions to a discourse-theoretical account of the unraveling of the regime's commonsense. In the present context, that means freeing Laclau and Mouffe's best insights from the post-Marxian blinders that distorted their initial reception and resituating them in a broader, neo-Marxian framework.

To this end, consider how their notion of "hegemonic articulation" might clarify the recent and ongoing breakdown of neoliberal commonsense. Like its social-democratic predecessor, this hegemonic nexus interwove interpretations of two different aspects of right or justice: a *distributive* module, focused on the norms that should govern "the economy," especially those allocating income and jobs, and a *recognition* module, concerned with the values that should underpin the status order, especially those conferring membership and respect. Such understandings were among the basic building blocks of neoliberal commonsense, but they were articulated in two different ways.

Progressive neoliberalism combined upward redistribution through financialization with meritocratic-individualist recognition. Promising to admit "talented" women, gays, and "minorities" to the ranks of corporate management, it deployed liberal, capital-friendly memes of "diversity" and "merit" to cast an emancipatory veneer over an economic agenda designed to benefit cognitive capital (finance, IT, media, and entertainment) at the expense of manufacturing and of working-class people in general, all the while boasting of its cosmopolitan concern for "the global poor." This strain of neoliberalism prevailed in many countries of capitalism's historic core, where it successfully hegemonized mainstream currents of progressive social movements, such as feminism and anti-racism. The effect was to inflect such movements as "globalist" and "elitist," hostile to national working-class fractions reeling from deindustrialization.

But progressive neoliberalism was contested, and at times defeated, by a rival bloc. *Reactionary neoliberalism* promoted an equally plutocratic agenda. While claiming to foster small business and manufacturing, its true economic project centered on bolstering finance, military production, and extractive energy, all to the principal benefit of the global

1 percent. What was supposed to render that palatable for the base it sought to assemble was an exclusionary politics of recognition. Bent on distinguishing itself from a progressive competitor tarred as globalist and elitist, reactionary neoliberalism mimicked the accents of the "common man": ethnonationalist, anti-immigrant, and pro-the majority's religion—whether Christianity or Hinduism, Judaism or Islam.

The opposition between progressive and reactionary neoliberalisms structured the hegemonic field in many countries for several decades. Fierce though they were, their battles hardly ever touched basic questions of political economy. Sectoral differences aside, both blocs supported "free trade," low corporate taxes, curtailed labor rights, the primacy of shareholder value, winner-takes-all compensation, and financial deregulation. Both elected leaders who sought "grand bargains" aimed at "flexibilizing" labor markets and cutting entitlements. The key differences between them did not concern distribution, but recognition.

As a result, the political commonsense of the preceding period was highly restrictive. Granted, voters could choose between multiculturalism and ethnonationalism. But they were stuck, either way, with financialization and deindustrialization. With the menu limited to progressive and reactionary neoliberalisms, the political universe excluded narratives that opposed the decimation of working- and middle-class standards of living. And that left a *gap* in the hegemonic field: an empty, unoccupied zone, where anti-neoliberal discourse might have taken root. Given the accelerating pace of deindustrialization; the proliferation of precarious, low-wage McJobs; the rise of predatory debt; and the consequent decline in living standards for the bottom two-thirds, plus the systematic hollowing out of public power, it was only a matter of time before someone would proceed to occupy that empty space and fill the gap.

That is precisely what the various "populisms" now proliferating have proceeded to do. These, too, articulate distributive norms with recognition values; and they, too, differ among themselves. *Reactionary populists* combine "antiglobalist" views of recognition with distributive ideals aimed at supporting (the "right" kind of) families, in effect, strict immigration controls for "outsiders" plus generous social provision for "insiders." By contrast, *progressive populists* join inclusive views of recognition with egalitarian ideals of distribution: in a nutshell, opposition to gender, racist, and anti-immigrant violence plus job creation and financial reform. Thus, both types of populism excoriate "the rigged economy" and appeal to "the people." Increasingly, too, both claim to speak for "the working class." But they interpellate the latter in different terms. The reactionary populist view is traditional and narrow: "workers" are white, straight, male, and Christian, based in mining, drilling, construction, and heavy industry. By contrast, the progressive populist view is more expansive, encompassing not only factory operatives, but also agricultural, domestic, public-sector, and service-sector workers, who are often women, migrants, and people of color. The resulting battle of populisms turns largely on the definition of political community. The litmus test, increasingly, is migration.

Here, then, is the current field, as viewed through the "hegemonic articulation" lens of Laclau and Mouffe. At the moment, the reactionary populists have the upper hand. Yet their exclusionary politics of recognition prevent them from forging a broad subaltern bloc with sufficient political heft to defeat the neoliberals in the longer term. Only progressive populism has the chance to accomplish that and thus to point toward an emancipatory resolution of the present crisis. But it faces some formidable competition—and not only from its reactionary-populist counterpart. Equally if not more perilous are the concerted efforts now under way to revive progressive neoliberalism in a new guise. Faced with the populist threat, partisans of global finance seek to convince progressives of every stripe, including progressive populists, to close ranks with their liberal "protectors." Warning of "the return of fascism," they insist that egalitarians abandon their ambitious projects of social transformation and work instead to restore the status quo ante, which means resurrecting the very arrangements that created all manner of Trumpisms across the globe. They seek in effect to hegemonize progressive populism, to harness the latter's forces for their own neoliberal agenda, now repackaged as militantly anti-racist and "antifascist." The aim, in other words, is to reorganize the field of hegemonic struggle, eliminating progressive populism as an independent force and simplifying the map into a single sharp opposition between two and only two options: progressive neoliberalism or reactionary populism.[8]

This much is clear when we connect Laclau and Mouffe's conception of hegemonic articulation to a structural account of the present institutional crisis of financialized capitalism. Equally clear are the outlines of another possibility. Progressive populists might decline the invitation to join with progressive neoliberals against reactionary populism. Pursuing a different line of attack, they might seek to build an alternative counterhegemonic bloc through a strategy of *double separation*. Rejecting not only reactionary populism but also progressive neoliberalism, they might try to split both of those blocs and win over fractions of each to a new alliance, premised on egalitarian distribution and inclusive recognition. In the case of progressive-neoliberalism, the aim would be to separate the mass of working-class women, immigrants, and people of color from the lean-in feminists, from the meritocratic anti-racists and anti-homophobes, and from the corporate-diversity and green-capitalism shills who hijacked their concerns and inflected them in capital-friendly terms. With respect to reactionary populism, the idea would be to separate working-class communities from the forces promoting militarism, xenophobia, and ethnon-ationalism that style themselves defenders of the "common man" while promoting plutocracy on the sly. By winning over the working- and middle-class fractions of both of those pro-capitalist political blocs, progressive populists might build an anticapitalist force that is large and powerful enough to transform society.

The chances for achieving this outcome may appear slim. But to discount them entirely would be to foreclose histori-cal possibility through self-fulfilling prophecy. In sketching the outlines of this scenario here, I have drawn on a reading of *Hegemony and Socialist Strategy* that diverges from the one that guided many new leftists of my generation to post-Marxian discursive idealism. In my reading, the book's account of hegemonic articulation can itself be fruitfully articulated with a structural-institutional critique of finan-cialized capitalism. Today, in other words, we can articulate its ideas to another Marxism, a Marxism that avoids the class essentialism so skillfully criticized by Laclau and Mouffe. This Marxism would combine their stress on the importance of counterhegemony, as opposed to mere opposition, with an account of the institutional context that demands it today. Analyzing hegemony as capitalist strategy, this framework would also clarify how a radical challenge to financialized capitalism might emerge. It is a Marxism that aspires both to honor Laclau and Mouffe's insights and to overcome their blindspots.

Notes

1. The present chapter originated as a lecture delivered at the conference on "Hégémonie, populisme, émancipation: perspectives sur la philosophie d'Ernesto Laclau" (Hegemony, Populism, Emancipation: Perspectives on the Philosophy of Ernesto Laclau), Paris, May 26, 2015.

2. Although they are not the focus of the present chapter, my perspective also identifies relatively autonomous and equally deep-seated tendencies to crises of social reproduction and of ecology. For an account that includes those "contradictions" as well, see Fraser 2014.

3. I use the expression "financialized capitalism" to designate the current regime of capitalism as an institutionalized social order. Like its counterpart expression "state-organized capitalism," this one names a distinctive, historically specific way of institutionalizing capitalism's constitutive divisions among polity/economy, economic production/social reproduction, and society/nature. By contrast, I use the term "neoliberalism" to designate the hegemonic commonsense of that social order, whose core assumptions naturalize the basic presuppositions of financialized capitalism.

4. For an account of the pervasiveness of financial flows through virtually all social spaces and institutions in the current regime, see Lapavitsas 2014.

5. For diagnoses that utilize such terms, see Brown 2006 and Crouch 2004.

6. The principal exception is the United States, which can simply print more of the dollars that serve as "world money."

7. For a fuller analysis of the structural-institutional dimension of the present crisis of democracy, see Fraser 2019.

8. For a fuller analysis of the hegemonic dimension of the present crisis of democracy, see Fraser 2017.

References

Brown, Wendy. 2006. "American Nightmare: Neoliberalism, Neoconservatism, and De-Democratization." *Political Theory* 34, no. 6 (December): 690–714.

———. 2015. *Undoing the Demos: Neoliberalism's Stealth Revolution.* Brooklyn: Zone Books.

Crouch, Colin. 2004. *Post-Democracy.* Cambridge: Polity Press.

———. 2009. "Privatised Keynesianism: An Unacknowledged Policy Regime." *British Journal of Politics & International Relations* 11 (3): 382–399.

———. 2011. *The Strange Non-Death of Neoliberalism.* Cambridge: Polity Press.

Dardot, Pierre, and Christian Laval. 2013. *The New Way of the World: On Neoliberal Society.* Translated by Gregory Elliott. London and New York: Verso Books.

Fraser, Nancy. 2008. *Scales of Justice: Reimagining Political Space in a Globalizing World.* New York: Columbia University Press.

———. 2014. "Behind Marx's Hidden Abode: For an Expanded Conception of Capitalism." *New Left Review* 86 (March): 55–72.

———. 2015. "Legitimation Crisis? On the Political Contradictions of Financialized Capitalism." *Critical Historical Studies* 2, no. 2 (Fall): 157–189.

———. 2017. "From Progressive Neoliberalism to Trump—and Beyond." *American Affairs* 1, no. 4 (Winter): 46–64.

———. 2019. "Democratic Crisis as Capitalist Crisis: On the Political Contradictions of Financialized Capitalism." In *Was stimmt nicht mit der Demokratie? Eine Debatte mit Klaus Dörre, Nancy Fraser, Stephan Lessenich und Hartmut Rosa* (What's wrong with democracy? A debate among Klaus Dörre, Nancy Frasser, Stephan Lessenich and Hartmut Rosa), edited by Hanna Ketterer and Karina Becker, 77–99. Berlin: Suhrkamp Verlag.

Gill, Stephen. 1998. "New Constitutionalism, Democratisation and Global Political Economy." *Pacifica Review* 10 (4): 23–28.

Harvey, David. 2007. *A Brief History of Neoliberalism*. Oxford: Oxford University Press.

Laclau, Ernesto, and Chantal Mouffe. 1985. *Hegemony and Socialist Strategy: Towards a Radical Democratic Politics*. London: Verso Books.

Lapavitsas, Costas. 2014. *Profiting without Producing: How Finance Exploits Us All*. London: Verso Books.

Wood, Ellen Meiksins. 1981. *The Separation of the Economic and the Political in Capitalism*. *New Left Review* 1 (27): 66–95.

5

Feminism and the Anti-Trump Resistance

L. A. KAUFFMAN

Why is it that feminism has been relatively marginalized in the popular image of grassroots opposition to Trump and Trumpism in the United States? Why has "the resistance"— as it was so often termed—not typically been viewed or described as feminist, first and foremost, despite the central role of feminist organizing in the early days of this broad social movement, and the dominant role of women with feminist values in every aspect of its work?

The anti-Trump resistance was kicked off, of course, by a feminist mobilization—the Women's Marches, which took place on the day after the man who lost the popular vote in the 2016 election was inaugurated in January 2017. Many qualities set this mobilization apart from any prior one in U.S. history. An estimated 4.1 million people, mostly women, took part in 650 different marches that day. That scale was record breaking in several respects. The first was overall size: More Americans marched on January 21, 2017, than had ever marched on the same day before, even when adjusting for population growth. The second was geographic reach: Americans marched in more towns and cities than during any comparable prior coordinated mobilization. Moreover, many of the local Women's Marches broke turnout records for their communities. The character of the Women's Marches was distinctive too. There had been major feminist demonstrations before in the United States, most notably a series of massive pro-choice marches in the 1990s and early 2000s, but these were narrower in their focus and typically staged in one or two major cities. It was new for women to stage a broad, nationwide, explicitly feminist, multi-issue mobilization, as they did in such astonishing numbers in January 2017 (Kauffman 2018, 91).[1]

The period after the marches witnessed a major upsurge in protest, organizing, and activism to counter the right-wing populism exemplified by Trump, and again this women-led grassroots activity broke prior records for levels of engagement. More people by far took part in public demonstrations during Donald Trump's presidency than during any comparable period in U.S. history, even when adjusting for population growth, and protests took place in more locations across the country than they ever had before. Civic engagement of many other kinds—constituents calling their members of Congress, voter turnout in local and congressional elections, and volunteer get-out-the-vote work for the 2020 election—surged as well. Women led this progressive groundswell, forming a solid majority—and often, as many as 80 percent or more—of participants in every aspect of the sprawling decentralized resistance to Trump administration policies, whether it took the form of marching and rallying, engaging in grassroots lobbying, registering voters, or taking part in civil disobedience actions (Kauffman 2017; Fisher 2018; Shalby 2018; Hartig 2019). But neither these origins nor this composition has translated into a popular view of the resistance as foundationally feminist.

Feminism's erasure could be attributed, at least in part, to the workings of misogyny—that "hostile force field"—whose workings philosopher Kate Manne has analyzed so carefully (Manne 2018, 19). After all, the generative role of feminist organizing in past progressive movements has often been obscured or unacknowledged. Few remember, for instance, that it was militant suffragists who first staged organized protests at the White House—and who endured repeat jailing, forced labor, and forced feeding before establishing the now taken-for-granted right to picket there (Lumsden 1997). Recent scholarship has revealed how grassroots campaigns against sexual assault led by Rosa Parks and others paved the way for later civil rights organizing, but this influence is far from household knowledge (McGuire 2010).

That said, chance and human error play larger roles in history than we often want to acknowledge. In the case of the resistance to Trump, the relative invisibility of feminist influences on the movement writ large has much to do with the bumpy trajectory of the national organization that formed in the wake of the marches—Women's March, Inc.—and with a little-known incident that sharply limited its scope during the crucial period when the grassroots resistance was taking organizational form.

The Women's Marches famously began with posts on Facebook on Election Night 2016, by two white women who had no experience organizing marches. The posts spread virally on social media, above all in a massive secret Facebook group, Pantsuit Nation, associated with the Hillary Clinton campaign. No organization or coalition brought this groundswell into being; there were thousands of RSVPs before anyone had even begun to give thought to how a march, much less hundreds of marches, might be staged. The creator of one of the Facebook posts, New York fashion designer Bob Bland, quickly registered a new organization, Women's March, Inc., to coordinate the march in Washington, D.C., and women all around the country almost immediately stepped up to organize sister marches in their communities. Though many preexisting organizations would end up providing crucial logistical and other support to these mobilizations, the hundreds of Women's Marches around the country were all start-up events—self-organized, often by people who had little or no prior experience with political activism.

This quality was one of many that set the Women's Marches apart from prior grassroots mobilizations in the United States. "The Women's March was just so different from anything else that any of us have ever experienced," remarked Leslie Cagan, a veteran organizer who has probably coordinated more mass protests over the last half century than any other single person. "It wasn't only the numbers— you don't get those kinds of numbers unless you have a whole new grouping of people stepping up and taking action that have never done anything like that before."[2] There was simply no precedent for a grassroots-generated upsurge of this scale and breadth in recent U.S. history—and therefore no precedent for the challenging work that organizers and leaders within the movement encountered when seeking to translate the energy of mobilization into lasting impact.

Prior mass mobilizations in the United States, from the 1963 March on Washington for Jobs and Freedom (where Dr. Martin Luther King Jr. delivered his "I Have a Dream" speech) to the 2004 March for Women's Lives (a pro-choice march that drew well over a million participants, and may be the largest single protest event in U.S. history), have one thing in common: they have all been organized by coalitions of preexisting organizations. Sometimes, as with the 1963 march, the work of mounting the mobilization has been so draining for these organizations that it has left them depleted, weakening rather than enhancing their ability to organize afterward. James Farmer, the national chairman of CORE (the Congress of Racial Equality), a partner in the 1963 March, declared in 1967 that "the March sounded the death bell of the activist movement. Our chapters began to decline after the March and action began to decline" (quoted in Kauffman 2018, 53). The burst of energy and publicity associated with a major march often can't compensate for the exhaustion that organizers experience in its wake—it takes more work than most people realize to coordinate an event of this sort, and organizers are frequently too worn out in the immediate aftermath of a big mobilization to absorb or incorporate new participants into their work. On occasion, most dramatically with the 1982 march for nuclear disarmament, which was organized over the space of nineteen months and drew a million protesters to New York City, the process of mobilizing for a big demonstration spurred the creation of a significant number of new local groups whose work continued in the event's aftermath.[3]

But there has always been a coalition or organization driving the work. At least in the United States, no one before has ever tried to do it the other way around on anything like this scale: to build a lasting organization—or a movement comprising many organizations—out of an organic nation-wide groundswell.

Women's March Inc. found itself making major decisions in its early days with little time to gather input or deliberate. The organization's initial leadership team—a group of four co-chairs—were named through a process that was as improvisational and ad hoc as everything else about the movement in its inception. Bob Bland quickly heard emphatic feedback that the march organizers could not be all white like her and the small circle of early organizers she assembled. Michael Skolnik, a film producer and digital organizer with a strong interest in "leverag[ing] the power of celebrity" who was friends with a member of the initial team, recommended three seasoned women of color organizers, who agreed to take on the responsibility of serving as the organization's other co-chairs (Skolnik n.d.). Linda Sarsour, Tamika Mallory, and Carmen Perez had worked together on multiple previous occasions, including in 2015 when they jointly led a 250-mile march from New York to Washington in support of a package of progressive criminal justice legislation (Women's March Organizers and Condé Nast 2018, 37–53).

The diverse backgrounds of the co-chairs, and the expertise that Sarsour, Mallory, and Perez brought in issues like immigration and criminal justice that hadn't been centered by previous feminist movements, were widely heralded as an important step toward an inclusive and intersectional feminism. There was special power in the connections that the three women of color co-chairs brought to the legacy of Dr. Martin Luther King Jr. All three had been mentored or supported to varying degrees by King's longtime associate Harry Belafonte, who played a key role in organizing the 1963 March on Washington. Tamika Mallory had a long-standing relationship with Dr. Bernice King, the youngest daughter of the slain civil rights leader, who at Mallory's request gave her explicit blessing to naming the event the Women's March on Washington. Carmen Perez introduced the nascent organization to the Kingian principles of nonviolence, which became foundational parts of its identity. And Perez, Mallory, and Sarsour all had direct experience with nonviolent direct action in the King tradition, which uses disruptive methods of protest to magnify a movement's visibility, power, and impact.

All of these qualities made the fledgling Women's March organization an especially intriguing candidate to play a central leadership role in the opposition to Trump's right-wing populist policies. But the process of building their new organization, and seeking to provide leadership to a wider movement, was bumpy, to say the least. Among those who stepped up to stage and coordinate the first set of marches, there were political differences, personality conflicts, and turf wars, especially in the high-pressure early months. "The beauty of the Women's March was that lots of people came in to help and do things on the fly. So we didn't have time to build formal structures," observes Mrinalini Chakraborty, who served as Women's March National's national field director until mid-2018 and joined the organization's recon-stituted board of directors in 2019. But people didn't know each other or have time to build trust or anything more than the most rudimentary political alignment. "It was every-thing," she adds, referring to the challenges of the time, "the movement being new, the people being new activists, us try-ing to figure things out as things were running at a million miles per hour."[4]

Sophie Ellman-Golan, the director of communications and digital outreach for Women's March National in its first years, recalls that in the wake of the initial marches, "It was like an abundance problem. So much energy and so many people saying, 'What are you going to do next? We need you to do this. We need you to do that.'"[5] Most new organizations need to build their constituency; Women's March National came into being with one so massive—and so eager for guidance—that it was almost overwhelming. Not just march-ers but also the media were barraging the staff with ques-tions about future plans well before anyone had a chance to assess anything, much less have time to deliberate fully about planning. "We were having to make decisions overnight or over a matter of hours that typically you would spend six months figuring out," remembers outgoing national co-chair Bob Bland. "I think that we felt rushed because of the incredibly high amount of scrutiny that we were under by the national media, constantly reporting on every move, to come up with an answer about what's next. And that we actually didn't take the time to heal or to rest or to reflect."[6]

It is worth taking a moment to underscore what the leadership was able to do in its first two years. Women's March Inc. consistently upheld the ideal of a broad, multi-issue, multiracial feminist movement that centers the leadership of women of color, aspiring to move beyond past models of feminist organizing that sidelined questions of racial justice and the perspectives of marginalized women. And it did so with a base was that 70 percent white and initially filled with women new to organizing and activism. The organization elaborated an ambitious vision—through its Unity Principles, Policy Platform, and other initiatives—of sweeping changes, both cultural and legislative, that would reverse the damage of Trumpian populism and uplift women of all backgrounds and their communities. Women's March Inc. either led or supported many of the most noteworthy early protests against Trump administration actions, in some cases with little public credit. The organization, for instance, threw its weight behind the high-profile 2017 Muslim Ban protests at airports around the United States, helping create the image of a spontaneous rapid response to Trump's executive order by mobilizing its enormous base of marchers. It played a crucial behind-the-scenes coordinating role in the record-breaking student walkouts in response to gun violence in March 2018, in which more than 1 million students staged three thousand protests, across all fifty states. And it co-organized the largest women's civil disobedience actions in U.S. history, first against the Trump administration's cruel and abusive family separation policy and later during the Supreme Court confirmation process for antiwoman extremist Brett Kavanaugh.

But crucial organizing opportunities were lost along the way, especially during the early period of chaos. One little-known lost opportunity in particular dramatically limited the organizing reach of Women's March, Inc.—and paved the way for Indivisible, a different new resistance project that was not explicitly feminist, to become the leading organizational container for grassroots activism against Trump and Trump-ism, especially in the first two years of Trump's term of office.

The Women's March, Inc. team followed up on its initial January 2017 mobilization—and responded to the urgent requests for political guidance—by rolling out a series of ten recommended action steps beginning just after the marches. For the second of these, marchers all around the country were encouraged in February 2017 to gather in informal "huddles" of ten to fifteen people to discuss and plan next steps. The idea, explained Chakraborty, was "to create these really hyperlocal groups where people could take small or big actions. The idea was to keep them engaged."[7] The response to this step was extraordinary: more than 5,500 of these small groups were convened. They hearkened back to the small consciousness-raising groups that were hall-marks of the Women's Liberation Movement in the late 1960s and early 1970s, but on a much larger scale, and with central coordination. Had these local formations endured, it would have been by far the largest network of grassroots feminist groups ever seen in the United States—and one, moreover, with multiracial leadership and broadly intersec-tional politics.[8]

But almost as soon as they were formed, the huddles lan-guished, thanks to a conflict with the contractor who had control over the sign-up data. No one yet has done a thorough study of how the internal practices of progressive organizations have changed under neoliberalism, but the changes have been far-reaching. Whole areas of work that used to be handled by either paid staff or organizational volunteers are now routinely outsourced to specialized private firms or individual contractors. The logistics for a high percentage of Trump-era protests and marches in Washington, D.C., were handled, for instance, by one company: D.C. Action Lab, founded by a group of longtime grassroots organizers, which also worked as a contractor for Women's March Inc. to support other aspects of its operations. There are numerous specialized firms that handle media, social media, website creation and maintenance, and other key tasks for leading progressive organizations.

One such contractor was handling a variety of data for the nascent Women's March organization, including the data on the 5,500 huddles. Because of a dispute between the firm and Women's March, which no one will discuss on the record, Women's March had no ability to contact the huddle coordinators or communicate with them in any way, until so much time had elapsed that follow-up was effectively moot.

What happened to the huddles? No one has systematically tracked their trajectory, but first and foremost, they did not remain associated with Women's March Inc. to any significant degree. A very small number evolved into Women's March chapters. A sizable number no doubt disbanded, or more precisely, did not continue meeting. Strong anecdotal evidence suggests that a great many—maybe most—evolved into affiliates of Indivisible, the progressive advocacy project founded in December 2016 by two former congressional staffers. During the period in which Women's March Inc. was unable to communicate with its huddles, Indivisible rapidly mushroomed into a network of 6,000 local groups. Indivisible offered those who had been activated by the marches a clear road map for ongoing action, which was what the grassroots was craving.

It is impossible to know what difference it would have made if Women's March Inc.—instead of, or in addition to, Indivisible—had maintained primary ties with thousands of local groups. The robust local network that Indivisible created gave a congressional and electoral focus to the anti-Trump resistance that clearly helped sway the November 2018 midterms, and played an important role in the massive grassroots get-out-the-vote mobilization that led to Trump's 2020 electoral defeat. But affiliation with Indivisible also meant forgoing an explicitly feminist identity and politics in favor of one that was generically progressive.

Women's March Inc., meanwhile, was facing so many other internal challenges that it wasn't at all clear they would have been able to sustain such a large network even if they had had access to the huddle data. They had some success with chapter affiliates but on a dramatically smaller scale. A few dozen of the informal local groups that took responsibility for organizing local or state Women's Marches in 2017 decided to constitute themselves as local or state Women's March organizations—but again, for some time after the first mobilization, the national staff didn't have either a plan or the capacity to work closely with them. "Everything about Women's March is a little bit like you're trying to put the toothpaste in the tube," observed executive director Rachel Carmona, who came on staff in February 2018. The chapters, she noted, "existed before the thought to sustain them and support them existed, because they came into existence first."[9] Chapters formed even though there was no clarity about what it would mean to be a chapter, or how they would relate to the national organization.

It wasn't until 2018 that Women's March Inc. began to have anything like a consistent field operation to engage the sister marches or the chapters. By that point, many local groupings felt either distant or alienated from the national organization and one another. "Aside from the marches and [a late 2017] convention, chapters hadn't really had chances to interface with each other or to actually build serious relationships," observed Noor Mir of D.C. Action Lab, who began working with Women's March National on supporting and developing the chapter network in June 2018.[10] It was only at that point that Women's March National began holding weekly network calls, conducted a thorough field survey to hear the priorities and concerns of local organizers, and developed an affiliate agreement in collaboration with the chapters. It held its first, and to this date only, chapter convening in April 2019—more than two years after the first set of marches.

As chapters began to consolidate and stake out autonomous identities, a growing number of activists in the larger Women's March movement came to feel that the four national co-chairs were carrying forward not just the bold and empowering aspects of Dr. King's political legacy but also a more contested component: the model of charismatic, top-down leadership that he exemplified. Even in King's time, there were many people, especially Black women leaders in the civil rights movement, who criticized his organizing approach for failing to empower the grassroots or build robust movements that were not dependent on single individuals. Septima Clark, a Southern Christian Leadership Conference organizer who had created citizenship schools throughout the Deep South, wrote in her memoir about King's dismissive response when she urged him to adopt a more inclusive approach. "I sent a letter to Dr. King asking him not to lead all the marches himself but instead to develop leaders who could lead their own marches," she wrote. "Dr. King read that letter before the staff. It just tickled them; they just laughed" (quoted in Brown 1990, 77–78).

The hundreds upon hundreds of grassroots-organized sister marches in January 2017 had brought to life a version of Septima Clark's democratic vision. And at the national level, key Women's March organizers explicitly put forward a variation on her ideal. "Women's March is a perfect example of a leaderful movement," Janaye Ingram, the director of logistics for the 2017 D.C. march, declared not long afterward. "While we had four co-chairs who represented various communities, there were many other leaders at the table there to create something more beautiful and powerful than what any of us could ever have done" (quoted in Women's March Organizers and Condé Nast 2018, 53).

But it didn't feel that way at the grassroots, however—and it didn't play out that way over time. Women's March, Inc. didn't suffer from the problem of structurelessness so famously experienced by the collectives, consciousness-raising groups, and other small feminist formations of the early 1970s, where a lack of explicit agreements about decision-making processes tended to concentrate power in the hands of a few (Freeman n.d.). On the contrary, Women's March, Inc. had a very clear structure. It was one that gave all formal decision-making power to the four co-chairs, without mandating any broader participation or mechanisms of inclusion. That fact was not widely known, but the sense of concentrated power was communicated to the grassroots through the intense media spotlight on the four co-chairs, and the sense that the new leaders were basking too comfortably in it, by say, posing for the cover of *Glamour* while local organizers were already feeling sidelined and neglected. In the words of Caitlin Breedlove, a longtime organizer who was hired by Women's March National in early 2018 to evaluate and help transform its organizational culture, the grassroots struggled with "how to deal with something as distributed and big as the Women's March being credited to four individuals, any four individuals." She continued, "Many of the chapters feel that this board [the four co-chairs] jumped in front of a wave of people already in motion and claimed them and claimed ownership of them. And that will never work in organizing movements. Whether that was the intention or not, I think that's how marchers around the country have felt. Like, 'Who decided y'all were in charge?'" (With the answer seeming to be, quite awkwardly for an intersectional feminist movement: a white man.)[11]

The concentration of power, and lack of structures to hold the leaders accountable, shaped the way that a major leadership failure landed within the movement: how Women's March Inc. handled co-chair Tamika Mallory's public praise in spring 2018 for the anti-Semitic, homophobic, and transphobic Nation of Islam leader Louis Farrakhan. The co-chairs responded awkwardly and defensively; that, in turn, gave ammunition to conservative critics, who publicized the comments again many months later, in the wake of the October 2018 Tree of Life synagogue massacre, in a pointed effort to bring the organization down. Co-chair Carmen Perez wrote in an op-ed for *The Forward* several days before the 2019 marches, "I want to be unequivocal in affirming that the organization failed to act rapid[ly] enough to condemn the egregious and hateful statements made by a figure who is not associated with the Women's March in any way. This failure caused deep hurt and pain, especially because our movement is dedicated to centering inclusiveness" (Perez 2019). But this apology, like the other public statements from the Women's March condemning anti-Semitism, homophobia, and transphobia, itself came late.[12]

By that point, though, dozens of local march organizations had already declared they were disassociating from Women's March National. The weakness of Women's March field organizing was a contributing factor. Though this fact was never publicly known, only one of the breakaway chapters had been actively engaged in the chapter network and chapter calls; the others had been much more loosely affiliated, and had little relationship to the national organization beyond a listing on their website. With media attention focused exclusively on the Farrakhan controversy, few outside the organization were aware that Women's March National was already, in the words of Caitlin Breedlove, "reconfiguring the organization so that there was more ability to share power." In the months between Mallory's comments and the media firestorm, Women's March Inc. had been meeting with Jewish and LGBTQ leaders, along with many others in its network; surveying its chapters; beefing up its field operation; building its youth program; and taking other steps to relate more horizontally and effectively with key movement stakeholders.[13]

Women's March Inc. named a greatly expanded new board of directors in September 2019, and Mallory, Sarsour, and Bland stepped down, leaving just one of the original co-chairs—Carmen Perez—in the organization's leadership. Explained Omaima Khan, director of operations for the organization at the time, "The best thing we can do, I think, is really learn from our mistakes, and as the organization grows, we want our leadership to grow. And we want the model for that to look a little bit different and be a little more collaborative." The organization held a major feminist leadership gathering in Washington, D.C., on the heels of its modest January 2020 March on Washington, which took place in the midst of Trump's impeachment trial, and entered the period of the COVID-19 pandemic and the 2020 election almost as a new organization altogether.[14]

The Women's March organization did crucial work to safeguard women's rights and democracy in the first years of the Trump administration. The intersectional feminism it seeks to embody always had the potential to be not just the antithesis but a powerful antidote to the rise of authoritarian populism and the misogyny, white supremacy, xenophobia, homophobia, and other hatreds on which authoritarianism feeds. But ideas are not the same as organizing—and organizing weaknesses, more than any other factor, help explain why feminism became so sidelined in the popular image of the anti-Trump resistance, after a feminist mobilization kicked that resistance off.

Notes

Research for this essay was supported by the Wallace Global Fund. Kauffman has worked, beginning in 2020, as an editorial consultant and senior strategy advisor for Women's March Inc.

1. The data on Women's March crowd participation was compiled by the Crowd Counting Consortium, https://sites.google.com /view/crowdcountingconsortium/view-download-the-data; a chart comparing the January 21, 2017, mobilization with previous days of coordinated action can be found in Kauffman 2018.

2. Telephone interview with Leslie Cagan, May 29, 2019. Interview quotations have in some cases been condensed for length but have not otherwise been edited.

3. Cagan interview.

4. Interview with Mrinalini Chakraborty, Brooklyn, New York, March 28, 2019.

5. Telephone interview with Sophie Ellman-Golan, May 23, 2019.

6. Telephone interview with Bob Bland, May 23, 2019.

7. Chakraborty interview. The "Next Step Huddle Guide" from January 2017 is archived at https://docs.google.com/document/d /1KzjyVCo2aiwV9VnRP5tTyt9Dkmbg3DuuMNy9ocj3DeY /preview.

8. On the role of small groups in the Women's Liberation Movement, see Freeman (1975).

9. Interview with Rachel Carmona, Brooklyn, New York, May 16, 2019.

10. Telephone interview with Noor Mir, May 13, 2019.

11. Telephone interview with Caitlin Breedlove, May 10, 2019.

12. Coverage of the Farrakhan controversy was voluminous; see Stockman (2019) and Desanctis (2019).

13. Breedlove interview.

14. Interview with Omaima Khan, New York, New York, May 13, 2019.

References

Brown, Cynthia Stokes. 1990. *Ready from Within: Septima Clark and the Civil Rights Movement*. Trenton: Africa World Press.

Desanctis, Alexandra. 2019. "Top Sponsors Quietly Drop Women's March amid Anti-Semitism Allegations." *National Review*, January 14, 2019. https://www.nationalreview.com/corner/top -sponsors-quietly-drop-womens-march-amid-anti-semitism -allegations/.

Fisher, Dana R. 2018. "Who Came Out in the Brutal Heat to the 'Families Belong Together' March? Here's Our Data." *Washington Post*, July 3, 2018. https://www.washingtonpost.com/news /monkey-cage/wp/2018/07/03/who-came-out-in-the-brutal-heat -to-the-families-belong-together-march-heres-our-data/.

Freeman, Jo. 1975. *The Politics of Women's Liberation*. New York: McKay.

———. n.d. "The Tyranny of Structurelessness." JoFreeman.com. https://www.jofreeman.com/joreen/tyranny.htm

Hartig, Hannah. 2019. "In Year of Record Midterm Turnout, Women Continued to Vote at Higher Rates Than Men." Pew Research Center, May 3, 2019. https://www.pewresearch.org/fact -tank/2019/05/03/in-year-of-record-midterm-turnout-women -continued-to-vote-at-higher-rates-than-men/.

Kauffman, L.A. 2017. "The Trump Resistance Can Best Be Described in One Adjective: Female." *The Guardian*, July 23, 2017.

https://www.theguardian.com/commentisfree/2017/jul/23/trump
-resistance-one-adjective-female-womens-march.

———. 2018. *How to Read a Protest: The Art of Organizing and Resistance*. Oakland: University of California Press.

Lumsden, Linda J. 1997. *Rampant Women: Suffragists and the Right of Assembly*. Knoxville: The University of Tennessee Press.

Manne, Kate. 2018. *Down Girl: The Logic of Misogyny*. New York: Oxford University Press.

McGuire, Danielle L. 2010. *At the Dark End of the Street: Black Women, Rape, and Resistance—a New History of the Civil Rights Movement from Rosa Parks to the Rise of Black Power*. New York: Vintage Books.

Perez, Carmen. 2019. "Jewish Women Should Join Us at the Women's March Despite Our Mistakes." *The Forward*, January 15, 2019. https://forward.com/opinion/417568/jewish-women-should-join-us
-at-the-womens-march-despite-our-mistakes/.

Shalby, Colleen. 2018. "A Record Number of Women Are Running for Office: This Election Cycle, They Didn't Wait for an Invitation." *Los Angeles Times*, October 10, 2018. https://www.latimes
.com/politics/la-na-pol-women-office-20181010-story.html.

Skolnik, Michael. n.d. Personal Website. Accessed November 6, 2021. https://about.me/michaelskolnik.

Stockman, Farah. 2018. "Women's March Roiled by Accusations of Anti-Semitism." *New York Times*, December 23, 2018. https://www
.nytimes.com/2018/12/23/us/womens-march-anti-semitism.html.

Women's March. 2017. "Next Step Huddle Guide." https://docs
.google.com/document/d/1KzjyVCo2aiwV9VnRP5tTyt9Dkmbg3
DuuMNy9ocj3DeY/preview.

Women's March Organizers and Condé Nast. 2018. *Together We Rise: Behind the Scenes at the Protest Heard around the World*. New York: Dey Street Books.

6

Organizing for Power

The Grassroots Struggle for Inclusive Democracy

HEATHER BOOTH, JYL JOSEPHSON,
SCOT NAKAGAWA

We live in precarious times. Authoritarianism is on the rise here and abroad, and democracy is under threat. And yet we persist. In February 2020, the Institute for Research on Women at Rutgers University hosted a conversation among three leading activists, Heather Booth, Jyl Josephson, and Scot Nakagawa, about building grassroots political movements in an era of authoritarian populism. Each has dedicated their life to building democracy from the grassroots. Together they bring to the table a rich history of labor and community organizing and fighting for civil rights and social justice.

What first brought you into organizing? What are the issues you've been most involved in? What sustains you as an organizer?
Heather: Love got me into this. I grew up in a family which believed that love is at the center of what we do. I knew that

if you love people and hate injustice, we could take action in the world to try and make it better.

In 1964 I went to Mississippi as part of the Freedom Summer Project. In 1964, poor Black people in Mississippi were being terrorized. The crimes that were going on were invisible to the rest of the public because there was no way to get the message out. They recruited northern students to come down and support the courageous work being done in Mississippi. I was one of those students. I was eighteen years old. I was in college at the time.

The Summer Project gained notoriety because three young volunteers, Andrew Goodman, James Chaney, and Michael Schwarner, were killed at the hands of the Klan. While they were looking for the bodies of those three young men, they found the bodies of other Black men whose hands were bound or feet were chopped off and who were then thrown into the Tallahatchie or the Pearl River. Those disappearances hadn't even been reported because it was such a state of terror. When they found the bodies, they weren't investigated as murders. Years later, they were investigated as cold cases.

Black lives did not matter in Mississippi in 1964. But within a year, there was a Voting Rights Act. We made progress because people organized. I think it's important to underscore this because now we're in a period that is different in the peril and yet comparable in how terrorizing it is—and how threatening. The lesson I learned was that if you organize, you can change this world. But you need to organize, not only talk about it.

I also learned that sometimes you have to stand up to illegitimate authority. It was the first time I was ever arrested. I was holding a sign supporting voter registration, and I was arrested. The third big lesson I learned is that you need to trust local people. They know what they want. If you support them, their leadership will shine through. That's the story of how I came into this work. The guiding principles are to love people and hate injustice and take action that will make a difference.

Jyl: I came to organizing out of self-interest, as I think most of us do. One of the things that the organization I work with teaches is that you don't want people to lead an organization if their primary motivation is to help other people. Because people won't stay engaged in organizing if their primary motivation is to help other people.

I just finished reading Charles Payne's book, *I've Got the Light of Freedom* [about the Mississippi Freedom Project]. One thing that's wonderful about Charles Payne's book is that he really tells you the stories of all the local African Americans who had been organizing for decades and trying to get something to happen. He describes the way that power operates. One of the lessons—and I'll keep saying this—is that you get as much justice as you have the power to compel. It doesn't matter that your cause is right. You have to have the power to make it happen.

I've mostly worked with two different kinds of organizations. When I was living in Texas more than twenty years ago, my older son came out to me. He was thirteen. We were living in Lubbock, Texas, and it was not a time when it was safe to be out in school. I got involved with the local PFLAG chapter, which used to stand for Parents, Family and Friends of Lesbians and Gays. Now it's an umbrella term that includes all LGBTQ folks. The first time I went to talk to a state legislator in Texas was when we were trying to prevent the state Defense of Marriage Act (DOMA) from being passed. This was just a couple of years after the national DOMA was passed and states were also passing DOMAs to ban same-sex marriage. And our local legislator was key to blocking it.

Equality Texas, the umbrella organization, organized the PFLAGs to go and talk to state legislators. That was the first time I lobbied, even though I already had a PhD in political science. I went with my son, who was fifteen at the time. It was a wonderful experience to do that together, even though we weren't really listened to. Still, it was important to do that work.

The other kind of work that I got involved in, in Texas, was with an organization called West Texas Organizing Strategy. We were trying to get the state legislature to pass the Children's Health Insurance Program. It was very simple. Are you going to pass it and are you going to have the maximum number of children included? We went and lobbied our legislators and eventually we were able to get the legislation passed. Those are very small things. And yet justice doesn't happen in large sweeps. It happens when you organize people, relationally, locally. You get to know each other and build your power through relationships with other people.

There is a whole network of organizing that happens throughout the country. The organization that I now work with in Jersey City is affiliated with the Industrial Areas Foundation, where Heather trained early on with Saul Alinsky. The Highlander Center, where Scot used to work, also trained many of the leaders.

Scot: I got involved in community advocacy when I was really young. I was born and raised in two rural communities, one that was originally a pineapple workers camp, and the other an active sugar plantation in Hawaii. My parents and their parents before them worked in agriculture for at least part of their careers, were active in unions, and involved in election politics, so I grew up in a family and a community where organizing and elections work was a familiar and very ordinary part of everyday life. People worked, for the most part, for the same company, shopped at the same grocery stores, and turned out en masse for community events. It never seemed to me that you had the option not to participate. But I never thought about politics as a vehicle for people to build power. I just thought, you participate, you represent yourself, and that's it.

When I was in middle school, a really huge thing happened for people in Hawaii: the Voyage of the Hokule'a, a National Geographic–sponsored journey of a traditional Hawaiian sailing canoe from Tahiti to Hawaii. That event, which proved that Polynesians were successfully navigating and engaging across further distances than Europeans for generations, was a complete surprise to a lot of us. We had been told the most horribly trivializing and racist stories about how Hawaiians accidentally ended up in Hawaii.

When that story got told, it became apparent to me for the first time that we had been lied to. There was no evidence for those other stories. It was a lesson to me in power, and about how power allows people to be able to define our stories, our narratives, and to determine who we are and how we see ourselves in the world.

That got me to turn to radical politics. I was no longer thinking, "I get on the phone and call people to get them to turn out on Election Day just because they're a Democrat or because our union endorsed them." I really started to question all the institutions around me, from the school I attended—to everything else.

I also grew up as a gay kid. I'm fifty-eight years old, so this is a long time ago. It was in the sixties when I first realized I was gay. I grew up in a very rural, culturally conservative community, and in a family that absolutely hated the idea that any of us would be gay, or even have sex outside of heterosexual marriage. I believed when I was in elementary school that if someone found me out, I might get killed, and the person that killed me might be a friend or loved one. I had this deep dark secret that I kept.

It eventually drove me out of my home. I found a community in Honolulu and did what homeless gay teens have to do to get by. That time of my life was a lesson in power and powerlessness that I will never forget.

I saw myself eventually working in agriculture, picking pineapples. But I took a detour, and used test-taking acumen to finish high school and become a tutor for GED candidates. Tutoring people who had dropped out or were pushed out of school was how I got a foothold in the community. From there it just snowballed into a bunch of other things.

That first little foothold eventually allowed me to create a career in community service, volunteer for community organizations, become involved in different kinds of community efforts, and to learn from people who were leading campaigns about how to build organizations and make change happen. That's really where all this came together for me. It was by complete accident.

I wonder if each panelist could next share with us stories of the most significant campaigns you've worked on. What do you think made them successful? What can we learn from them?

Scot: When I was telling you that last story, the one thing I planned on sharing but didn't was about the way I got into organizing. It was not because I felt politically disenfranchised, though I was. It was because I wanted acknowledgment and respect. I wanted to be acknowledged as a whole human being and to be respected according to how I define myself.

In terms of the campaigns that I've been involved in since that time, the most successful ones actually center that idea. If you're hungry, there are easier ways to get fed than marching on your state capitol. But people do it because they want acknowledgment and respect. They want dignity. They want to be understood. They want to be seen as people who are deserving of a fair share of the wealth of this nation, and want fair participation in our political system because these are not just material necessities, but ways of being acknowledged and valued.

I've been involved in a number of campaigns on LGBTQ issues. I worked for a while for the National LGBTQ Task Force, and my job was to help people mount campaigns against right-wing-sponsored anti-LGBTQ initiatives. Those campaigns would translate into statewide organizing when people didn't just look at the dry politics and ask, "How do we get to 50 percent plus one?" but instead focused on how to build the kind of community that can sustain political work over time. All of that began with acknowledgment and respect.

In those days consultants would sometimes say to LGBTQ communities that were being attacked, "No National Coming Out Day," "No Pride parade," "Quiet down!" We found that the opposite turned out to be the most effective way to mobilize people and make lasting change happen. That was the biggest lesson for me.

Jyl: To answer the question of what campaigns I've worked on that have made a difference, I'm going to talk about water and dignity and respect. I live in Jersey City. I've lived in Jersey City for fifteen years now. I have two sons. One is grown, that I told you about already, and one is in fifth grade. When he was going into pre-K in our neighborhood school, we went into the building for the first time and the water fountains had police tape on them. I asked the teacher, "What's the story?" And she said, "Well, I've been here fourteen years and it's been that way the whole time."

Then I found out that it was throughout the city. There are about forty school buildings in Jersey City, and many of them are over a hundred years old. For about two decades there has been lead in the pipes, and the water fountains have been turned off, taped off. In some schools, the water fountains are off the walls, and so the district buys water in bottles. In some schools, you have to go to the social worker or the security guard to get a cup if you don't bring one to school. Now, water is a basic human right. And most of the schools in Jersey City don't have potable water in the drinking fountains. It's ridiculous. Many of the schools also do not have air conditioning. And there has been a regular problem with not enough water bottles being delivered, especially on hot days in September or in the early summer.

The organization that I work with organizes with more than thirty mostly religious organizations and other nonprofits from throughout Jersey City around water. Yesterday, we got a victory at two schools. At McNair High School and Public School 15 the water fountains have now been certified.

What happened was that the City said the schools were responsible, the schools said the City was responsible, and the Municipal Utilities Authority said that everybody else was responsible. These three public bodies were all pointing their fingers at somebody else. It took our organizing for several years to get to the point where we have water in a couple of schools. It's ridiculous that we have to fight for this. It's a long-term battle because it's going to take a couple more years to get it to every school.

Heather: What I find most interesting about the story is that for fourteen years this condition went on and people just assumed that you couldn't change it. Then they decide to organize. Things that we take for granted—that there's clean water, that there's electricity, that there's public education, that there's supposed to be an eight-hour workday—all things that make life bearable are only there because people organized for them at some point. To keep them and to expand them, we need to organize.

One of the main reasons that people don't continue to organize is they feel the struggle might not be worth the effort. Often, we don't treat each other well, even within our organizations. In the civil rights movement, there was a phrase: "Building a beloved community." I think we have to find ways to build and reflect that beloved community, to treat each other with dignity and respect, to give recognition when people have done amazing work.

Is there a victory that was our greatest victory? I've been through a lot of different victories: The Consumer Financial Protection Bureau returned $12 billion to consumers defrauded by companies. Women's rights have been transformed because we organized. I ran the campaign on marriage equality around the Supreme Court decision. Before that campaign there were at least eight statewide ballot measures where we lost. Then we began to organize and talk with people and hear their concerns, and respond and engage with them with dignity and respect. And we won.

I want to mention a campaign where we lost on the issue, but we are building the power that will eventually win. I was a senior adviser to the Immigration Reform Campaign. We did not get a pathway to citizenship for 11 million people. But we did transform how the immigrant community, itself, stands up and speaks with a new confidence. We've changed what leadership thinks in many places, and the vast majority of the American public—70 percent of the American public—believe that there should be a pathway to citizenship. Probably a higher percent believe that children shouldn't be separated from their parents.

We didn't win legislation, which we need. There are three things that combine for that kind of win. One is that you build the organized power of people, not just those who already agree. We need to be unified. We need to have our spirits raised and also to talk to those who are not confident that they can take action.

Second, we need political power. We've got 70 percent for a pathway to citizenship in the United States, 70 percent for not overturning *Roe v. Wade*, and 70 percent for almost every important issue in a decent and caring society. Yet each issue is pushed back because we haven't got political power.

Third, you make the greatest change when you hit a moment, and there is a movement, and there is a spark, and you can build organization within that framework. We can't determine when the movement will come, but when it does we can seize that energy and build on it.

The last thing I'd say is that we generally teach three principles at the Midwest Academy (wwwmidwestacademy .com), a training center for organizers. One, you actually want to win real victories that improve lives so that people know the struggle is worth the effort. Second, you want to give people a sense of their own power by fighting and winning not by having a benevolent university or corporate head or administrator give you something. Third, we change the structural relations of power so that we are stronger for the fights ahead.

What are the biggest threats to democracy today? How do we address them and build people-centered movements for justice in this moment of authoritarian populism?
Jyl: What I'm talking about is relational organizing. One of the biggest tools for relational organizing is a one-on-one meeting where you get to know another person not as a friend, but as a member of the public—you're getting to know what their values are, what their self-interest is, and whether they're someone you can engage with in building

power. The other thing we do is listen. We didn't decide we were going to organize around affordable housing or schools—we listened.

What are people worried about? Affordable housing (both rental and homeownership), public education, and then safety, and we are starting to organize on criminal justice now. Why do I mention this in the context of threats to democracy? Because I think one of the biggest threats to democracy is the way that we don't necessarily know our neighbors. If we don't know our neighbors, we can't engage with them in making our communities the kind of communities we want to live in.

This style of organizing teaches people how to build relationships through institutions. That can be difficult. A lot of people don't want to get involved with religious organizations, for example. One of the struggles we've had organizing around education is that a lot of parents and folks in schools are not necessarily connected to religious institutions. And on the other hand, a lot of our religious institutions are not necessarily connected to the schools, partly because of the history of Catholic schools in Jersey City.

We have had to work hard to build power across those organizations. It's taken several years but now we've got parents coming and talking to pastors—and these are parents who are almost allergic to religion, but they know that they have a common self-interest with some of the churches.

People build democracy together, and most of it takes local level, long-term organizing. I know people in Jersey City that I would never have known if I were not involved in this kind of organizing. I'm going to lift up Reverend Alonzo Perry, who is pastor of New Hope Missionary Baptist Church and is brilliant. I've been in meetings with the mayor with Reverend Perry present, and it's not clear that the mayor likes either of us, but he does respect us and the organization we represent. As leaders, we are able to work together because we know each other and trust each other, and we've been part of building an organization together.

I think the biggest threat to democracy is that we don't know each other. One of the best things we can do is build relationships in our local community through institutions and with our neighbors.

Scot: Every time I get that question, I have to take a breath because I have such bad news. For the last thirty years or so of my activist life, I primarily focused on fighting the Right. It started in 1988, when a young Ethiopian man in Portland, Oregon, named Mulugeta Seraw was murdered by neo-Nazi skinheads. It has continued through the years, focusing on religious right-wing groups attacking abortion rights and LGBTQ communities, and the emergence of white nationalism as a predominant politic on the white Right.

I view the rise of white nationalism as a tremendous threat to democracy, like the mainstreaming of Christian nationalism. Both movements have become popular fronts for right-wing corporate power. For that reason, they have a direct line into the Republican Party, which is something that most pro-democracy activists don't have into the Democratic Party. This means that they have the ability to amplify their voices and their policy positions tremendously.

History tells us that center-right coalitions are necessary to defeat right-wing takeovers. But the center-right has never been a friend of the Left, and the Left has never been a friend to the center-right, for very good reasons. That potentially makes the 2020 elections a lose–lose proposition for progressives. The white nationalist Right can pivot from the ballot to the bullet very easily. They have already proven their worth to the business Right by being a key block in the election of

Donald Trump. They are slowly merging with the Christian Right and becoming one singular movement that would be more significant in power than the Christian Right has been until now. That's my assessment. That's a terrible threat to democracy that all of us must address. But the world is not one in which right-wing white people rise up in insurrection and take over our government and the rest of us innocently stand by going, "oh, no." We who are witnessing the rise of authoritarianism aren't just innocent bystanders. There's a powerful authoritarian impulse all around us—right, left, and center—that the rise of right-wing authoritarianism is inspiring. I think this overall effect is the greatest threat to democracy.

I'm going to tell you a really quick story that I've been using with groups lately to help them understand what I mean. You understand what happened in China when the coronavirus first broke out? The government of China immediately imposed quarantines. People could not move. Viral outbreaks are one of the most likely early effects of climate change. We are unprepared for them. Our public health infrastructure has not been invested in for some time. We have a weak and overly expensive health care system in the United States. As these viral outbreaks happen, there's a possibility that there will be quarantines of different kinds and a culture of fear that develops where people start to tell on one another because so-and-so has a cold but hasn't gone to the doctor. That creates the context in which authoritarians can seize power by popular demand.

I also ask people, "Don't you love the Marvel movies?" "Didn't you love *The Black Panther*?" "Didn't you love *The Avengers*?"—I remind them that those are authoritarian narratives. If Spiderman was a real dude, he would be a total ass because he would have so much power. We project ourselves onto people like these characters because they speak to a deep insecurity we have. They can solve the problem. They can crack down on crime. They can fix this terrible injustice, not through collective action, but through the sheer will of individuals—and in some cases, like with Iron Man, through the use of technologies. When people disengage from one another, it allows that kind of thing to happen. That, to me, is the biggest threat to democracy. It's what keeps me up at night and gets me up at five o'clock in the morning to go to work.

Heather: To the question of what's the greatest threat to democracy, I have three thoughts. The greatest danger is not only Trump—but the forces that he represents and encourages, based on racism and antiscience, and in opposition to a government that can bring us together and represent our shared interests. Did you know that he dismissed the branch of government that had the people to work against pandemics like coronavirus? He did it as a budget cut. There are people who don't want to pay money to have a government or world that works for anyone else but them, and they've got enough money, so they don't really care.

The second threat to democracy is unaccountable, particularly corporate, power that is largely now funding right-wing and authoritarian organization. The Koch brothers don't want to pay money in taxes, and so they fund things to prevent this, even if it sparks anti-immigrant feelings or a populist reaction like, "We can blame the people below us. It's their fault. Or we can blame the Jews, or we can blame the Asians or we can blame the Muslims, or the women." I think this question of unaccountable power and tying it to a resilient right wing is key.

The third level of threat to democracy is our lack of confidence. Everything in this society tells us, "You're not good enough, you don't know enough, you're not smart enough, you're not pretty enough, you're not tall enough, you're not enough." When, in fact, we *are* beautiful. We *are* enough.

And we have the stuff that it takes. Thor or Iron Man can inspire us, but we need to take collective action and believe in ourselves, and believe in each other, and build those relationships, and organize to change the world.

Authoritarianism and organized racism are growing threats domestically as well as internationally. To many of us it seems very overwhelming and beyond our control. What do you think we should be doing to fight these worrying trends and to work toward building a more democratic future?

Scot: I recently did some training with a network of Asian progressive organizations in the Philippines. There are progressive parties in places like Thailand, India, and the Philippines, all of which are facing authoritarian governments. They brought me to the training because they thought that we had a magic bullet, that people in the United States knew how to defeat authoritarianism because they saw Donald Trump rising in popularity and yet failing in some ways to move his agenda because of the courts.

I had to bring them bad news. I said that I'm not sure that our grassroots resistance to Trump is having the effect we would like it to have yet. But our courts have had a very powerful effect in reining him in. It's really important for us to think about those democratic institutions that we have on our side that limit the power of the executive and that put checks and balances on that office, and to mobilize to protect them. It is the relative strength of democratic institutions in the United States that makes the definitive difference, not mass movements and popular dissent.

We know that Trump is appointing many judges. This is a terrible scenario. The people he's appointing would make your eyeballs fall out of your head. They are people who don't believe in government, much less liberal government. Some view our democratic institutions as impediments to the authoritarian society they want to create. They want to subvert or destroy these institutions. We need to start to monitor and respond to this.

We also need to recognize that law enforcement agencies, particularly in rural areas, are often influenced or taken over by white nationalist organizations. Key organizations include the 3 Percenters and the Oath Keepers, with a core membership of former first responders and military veterans.

The 3 Percenters is a paramilitary, white nationalist organization that believes that it took only 3 percent (or less) of the American population to mount the American Revolution. They believe that if they can get 3 percent in their corner, they can do it again.

The Oath Keepers are a similar type of organization. There's also the Constitutional Sheriffs and Peace Officers Association, which is a white nationalist organization that often works directly with rural county sheriffs' offices. These groups are all influenced to one degree or another by an American tradition of cynicism toward the federal government that is best articulated by something called the Posse Comitatus, which is Latin for power of the county. The Posse Comitatus is a historical organization that serves as a sort of ideological template for the groups out there now. This ideology informed the Bundy family's political views about the federal government, and their decision to resist federal authority, first in an armed standoff in Nevada in 2014, and then by taking over and occupying a federal bird sanctuary in Oregon in 2016.

White nationalist organizations are working with sheriff's offices to convince them that liberals are trying to take away guns. They want to convince county law enforcement that they have a legitimate constitutional right to be the ultimate arbiter of power in their counties. If liberals want to take your guns, your job is to protect gun rights, is the general logic. But it doesn't stop there. Gun rights advocacy is a soft entry point into even more dangerous political ideas.

They are also taking advantage of power voids in places that are suffering from huge revenue shortages—rural Oregon, for example, where 911 service is not available 24 hours a day in some places, and fire departments have been unfunded—and offering themselves as volunteers. They're culturally more similar to police officers and law enforcement agents all across the country (who are Republican registered in the majority), and they are also equipped to play some of these roles. They're like Isis—they go where there are power voids. When the Bundys were active in Oregon, in fact, people referred to them as Vanilla Isis. They were going into places where there was a power void and trying to take over.

Police accountability is hugely important. We need to recognize that there's an increasing impulse among progressive organizers, particularly in the generations below me, who want to disengage from the police. But we are paying for those police salaries with our tax dollars. They owe us something. They are part of government. Government must maintain a monopoly on violence. In other words, they are the only body within the United States that can legitimate the use of violence with impunity. That is our theory of law and order, like it or not.

The white nationalists are challenging that monopoly on violence. If governments do not respond appropriately, violent conflict can quickly envelop civil society. We need to move law enforcement into our corner as we were able to do after 1995 by engaging in strategic nonviolence. Also, we can't take our eyes off of law enforcement. The state has often used violence unjustly in North America, particularly toward native nations. It has accommodated and thereby legitimated white supremacist violence, and violence against women, LGBTQ people, Jews, and other minorities throughout our history.

The white Right has targeted college campuses because they understand that leaders of the future are being developed there, and the campus community is particularly susceptible to that kind of appeal. They go to places where conservative students will feel picked on because they're out of the majority, and then organize them. They'll run people for student government in order to try to subvert those bodies to move their agendas. Groups like Turning Point USA and the American Identity movement have been particularly active. You are at ground zero in some ways as students and the opportunity to organize is here. Faculty should get organized, as well. And staff of college campuses should get organized too, and be the first bulwark against the incursions of white nationalists on campus.

What is the best way to organize and change minds in toxic and difficult situations?
Heather: Often, fear and intimidation and social ostracism can make people feel it's not even worth trying in an area that's hard. If you can find other people who share your views, and who may have been driven underground, then at least you have a reference for mutual support and caring and acknowledgment and dignity, like Scot was saying, and building relationships, like Jyl was saying, and so you are supported.

Next you need to figure out a plan. Are you trying to change a law? Do you want to draw people in for common support? I often think that when we protest, sometimes it's just for ourselves. But it's not enough, so have a plan of action. That's one of the things we teach up at Midwest Academy.

Third, there's a kind of relational organizing that both Scot and Jyl know deeply, that's worth studying. Because it's how you help identify people who are open to persuasion in an area in which you mostly need persuasion. There are some areas where you just have to convince people to be active.

There's a style of organizing called the deep canvass, and you can see some examples of it online. I'm going to give you an example that was done on LGBT issues by a group initially out of California, after these statewide ballot measures were lost so repeatedly. Dave Fleischer first came up with it, but now there are many other people who work on this.

They do it in pairs, actually with someone videotaping so they can learn from what happened. You have to get trained on how to do it. You go door-to-door and maybe one in ten people will respond to you, initially. Some will slam the door. They'll say, "Who the hell are you?"

You say, "I'm with the community organization from wherever you said you were, and we're trying to talk to people about marriage equality." That's what was done, but it could be any issue.

"First, I'd want to ask you, are you willing to talk with me and my friend here? This is her name. Here's our story. And we'd like to videotape so that we can learn. Is that okay?"

If they say no, we don't videotape.

And you say: "I want to talk to you about marriage equality. Will you discuss that with me?"

And they say, "Sure, I hate it. The queers should all be locked up."

And you say: "So on a score of 1 to 10, I'm just going to write down—where 1 is being for it and 10 is being against it, what would you be?"

"I'm a 10."

And you say: "I want to tell you my story about what happened to me." You tell your story very briefly, maybe for three minutes.

And then you say, "Have you ever faced a situation where someone you knew was being mistreated and they had no place to go? Maybe they lost their job or felt threatened and they were so sad, and no one was there to support them? And all they wanted to do was to have a regular life. They felt so alone. Have you ever felt a situation like that?"

And you wait. Maybe one in ten people respond and say, "I did. I had a situation like that. My hand doesn't work right. They called me a gimp. My brother's Mexican and he was adopted . . ." People have a story to tell you, a relational story. You talk it through and maybe it takes 15 minutes. Maybe 20 minutes.

You say, "I want to ask you, again, where 1 is support and 10 is opposition, where would you be on marriage equality, now?" Of the people who were talked to, the vast majority changed their minds. Many saying: "I'd say I'm a 3, now. Thank you for talking to me."

I've seen this done on abortion, on immigration, on other issues. But you need training for it. The main thing I'm saying is, find a core group to support you, create a plan of action, and then there are ways to do persuasion.

Scot: There are examples in rural Oregon, and a group called the Rural Organizing Project (ROP) that has done some very, very effective work. A woman named Marcy Westerling who was an old ACORN (Association of Community Organizations for Reform Now) organizer founded ROP. It is active in all the rural counties in Oregon, some of which are very sparsely populated, very white nationalist as a legacy of Oregon's white supremacist history.

The way in which people have been able to address this is by beginning with the assumption that wherever there is an expression of hatred and authoritarianism, then there is also resistance. If you look, you will find the people, and those people will want to do something. They have proven this is right over and over and over again. I would begin there. Find out who's like-minded, who's interested in resistance, so that you're not standing by yourself.

In the eighties, when I lived in Portland, Oregon, neo-Nazi skinheads were recruiting in the alternative music scene, and they dominated it. It became a super scary place for people. Depending on what band was playing, you might not want to go there unless you were prepared for a fight. We went into the music scene and wore "Fight Racism" T-shirts, organized Rock Against Racism concerts, and put up posters in order to polarize the scene and identify a base of resistance. We quickly discovered that Marcy's principle was right. That, in fact, there were many, many young people in the scene who were feeling bullied and picked on and who were disgusted by what these neo-Nazi skinheads were bringing. They organized themselves into two groups in Oregon, Anti-Racist Action against racist skinheads, and Skinheads Against Racial Prejudice. One of my jobs was to help facilitate their organizing and to support them as they became targeted by the police.

It's really important to monitor the people who are being the loudest to try to disrupt them, and, if you can, associate them with bigoted organizations that may be distasteful to people. Then you need to reframe the debates that they're bringing to the community in ways that diffuse the tensions they're trying to exacerbate. It's important to compete for their base of supporters by talking about the real issues that are affecting people in your community, with real solutions—and that means organizing.

Those are things that I think that you can do. I think it's also super, super important to remember that in a place like rural Oregon, the people who represent white nationalist beliefs are people's neighbors. They're Uncle Bob. They're your friend. They attend the same church as you. Just going after them and shaming them doesn't work.

In Bend, Oregon, I know a woman who ran for and won a city council seat. She found out that her opponent was an Oath Keeper, a white nationalist, and wanted to expose him. Her campaign team and other people around her quickly told her, "That guy cut a tree off my house when it fell last winter." That's how the community thinks of him, and so you can't begin there—you have got to begin with the issues. This is not about saying that some people are bad people. It's about saying that there are bad ideas and here are some better ones.

Heather: Also, it's important to personalize who we are. I breathe like you breathe. This is what I want in my life. I'm not going after you.

Jyl: I think that's crucial. It's about seeing the humanity in people who have bad ideas, and introducing other ideas.

The problem is that white supremacy is an ideology that's very powerful and that people believe in very deeply. They think it's the truth, even when what they're arguing makes no rational sense. That's because the ideology is so powerful and shapes our thinking.

There's an essay by Barbara Jean Fields that was published thirty years ago. She talks about the terrain of racist ideology in the United States that makes people have beliefs that are harmful to democracy. You're not necessarily going to convince your family. I've had many arguments with my brother who is a Trump supporter. He is not going to change his viewpoint. And yet, for me, it's important that I say, "This is harmful," not just to the country but to people that I love. I think that you can talk about the humanity of the people who are being dehumanized by the ideologies that are being reproduced.

Scot: One of the things people have found—I don't know how they know these things, but they do—is that individuals respond to those who are protectors in a really different way than to others. If they perceive that you will offer them protection, then they are much more susceptible to come over to your side.

There's an incident where a Muslim immigrant in Holland jumped into icy water to save a Dutch boy. People tried to stop him because they thought he would die in the icy waters. He managed to rescue the boy and return him to safety. It changed the attitude of many in the community about Arab Muslim immigrants. At least in the immediate community, many people changed their minds.

But you have to have the attitude—it begins with that attitude—that I am your protector, and that we are here for one another. My dad was a really difficult guy in a lot of ways. A product of his generation. But as long as he was physically able and until he finally got too ill and passed away, he drove a Meals on Wheels truck. People are so full of contradictions. I think you just have to try to make a connection.

Jyl: I just want to say, again, that you get as much justice as you have the power to compel. And power is built by building relationships with people—and you can have fun together while you're doing this kind of organizing. So, work with your neighbors to build power so you can get the things that you want.

Heather: I want to close with a quote from Frederick Douglass, who was a great abolitionist before and during the Civil War. One of his most famous quotes is, "Those who profess to favor freedom and yet deprecate agitation, are people who want crops without plowing up the ground, they want rain without thunder and lightning. They want the ocean without the roar of its many waters. The struggle may be a moral one, or it may be a physical one, or it may be both. But it must be a struggle. Power concedes nothing without a demand. . . . It never did, and it never will."

I hope for all of you, that you go out and join with others, build those relationships, and organize for power, for people. And then we'll turn this incredibly perilous time into a time of inspiration, and we'll look back and say, "Remember when we organized, and we changed the world?"

Thank you, panelists, for your wisdom and inspiration.

Acknowledgments

For almost fifty years, Rutgers University's Institute for Research on Women has been an internationally recognized home for feminist scholarship. We are very pleased that this volume launches the Feminist Bookshelf series, which collects cutting-edge feminist research presented at the IRW. We thank Rutgers University Press's editorial director, Kimberley Guinta, for helping to steer this volume from idea to reality. We are indebted to the scholars and activists who spoke as part of IRW's Distinguished Lecture Series and allowed us to publish their contributions in this volume. We also thank the fellows, visiting scholars, and affiliates who participated in the seminar on populism and its perils: Donna Auston, Basuli Deb, Diane Shane Fruchtman, Angelique Haugerud, Maria Hwang, Chie Ikeya, Ying-Chao Kao, Suzy Kim, Susan Marchand, Ileana Nachescu, Snežana Otašević, Sara Perryman, and Catherine Wineinger.

The Rutgers School of Arts and Sciences (SAS) provides ongoing funding for IRW's work. We extend our thanks to SAS and to Dean Michelle Stephens for her steadfast support of our programming. We are also grateful to current and recent IRW executive committee members: Tyler Carson, Asenath Dande, Kayo Denda, Anette Freytag, Chie Ikeya, Suzanne Kim, Suzy Kim, Sara Perryman, Nancy Rao, Kyla Schuller, Mary Trigg, Ethel Brooks, and Cat Fitzpatrick.

The polish and professionalism of our administrative assistant, Andrea Zerpa, makes our work possible. We are also grateful to her predecessor, Meliseta Shand. We thank Moazima Ahmad for her assistance formatting the bibliographies in this volume.

We are fortunate to be embedded in a university with a rich feminist community, including our nine sister units of the Institute for Women's Leadership Consortium, of which IRW is a member. Institute for Women's Leadership Director Rebecca Mark and our friends at the Center for Women's Global Leadership (CWGL) deserve special mention. We share our building with CWGL, and their grace and reciprocity are intrinsic to the success of our programming.

Arlene thanks Sarah Tobias for her intellectual savvy, feminist zeal, and good humor. Her dedication makes this book series, and everything else that IRW does, possible. She also thanks the Department of Sociology at Rutgers University, and finally, Cynthia Chris, for love and support.

Sarah thanks IRW director Arlene Stein for great collegiality and for nurturing the supportive space that is IRW—and for numerous rides from New Brunswick to Jersey City in life before lockdown. She thanks former IRW directors Dorothy Hodgson, Yolanda Martínez-San Miguel, and Nicole Fleetwood. Finally, she thanks her friends and family, especially Beth and Talila, for sustaining her through the first grim year of COVID-19 with music, dance, laughter, and love.

Notes on Contributors

AMRITA BASU is the Domenic J. Paino Professor of Political Science and Sexuality, Women's and Gender Studies at Amherst College. Her scholarship explores women's activism, feminist movements, and religious nationalism in South Asia. Her most recent monograph, *Violent Conjunctures in Democratic India* (2015), shines a spotlight on when and why Hindu nationalists engage in violence against religious minorities. She is the author of *Two Faces of Protest: Contrasting Modes of Women's Activism in India* (1992) and the editor or coeditor of *Women's Movements in the Global Era: The Power of Local Feminisms* (2010, 2016); *Beyond Exceptionalism: Violence, Religion, and Democracy in India* (2006); *Localizing Knowledge in a Globalizing World* (2002); *Appropriating Gender: Women's Activism and Politicized Religion in South Asia* (1998); *Community Conflicts and the State in India* (1997); *The Challenge of Local Feminisms: Women's Movements in Global Perspective* (1998); and *Women, Gender and Religious Nationalism in India* (forthcoming, 2022). Amrita's research has been supported by the National Endowment for the Humanities, Social Science Research Council, John D. and Catherine T. MacArthur Foundation, Ford Foundation, Woodrow Wilson National Fellowship Foundation, and the American Institute of Indian Studies. She has served on the editorial boards of the *American Political*

Science Review; International Political Science Review; Inter-national Feminist Journal of Politics; Meridians: Feminism, Race, Transnationalism; and *Critical Asian Studies* and was the South Asia editor for the *Journal of Asian Studies.*

HEATHER BOOTH is one of the leading strategists for progres-sive issue and electoral campaigns. Her work as an organizer began in the civil rights, anti–Vietnam War, and women's movements of the 1960s and continues through today. She created JANE, an underground abortion service, before *Roe v. Wade* was successfully argued before the Supreme Court. She was the founding director and is now president of the Midwest Academy, training social change leaders and orga-nizers. She has been involved in political campaigns, includ-ing as the training director for the Democratic National Committee. In 2000, she was the director of the NAACP National Voter Fund, which helped to increase African American election turnout. She was the lead consultant, directing the founding of the Campaign for Comprehen-sive Immigration Reform in 2005. In 2008, Booth was the director of the Health Care Campaign for the AFL-CIO. In 2009, she directed the campaign to pass President Obama's first budget. In 2010, she was the founding direc-tor of Americans for Financial Reform, fighting to regulate the financial industry. She was the national coordinator for the coalition around marriage equality and the 2013 Supreme Court decision. She was strategic adviser to the Alliance for Citizenship (the largest coalition of the immigration reform campaign). She was the field director for Americans for Tax Fairness to stop the tax cuts for millionaires that may lead to cuts in Medicare, Medicaid, and education. She was the Progressive and Seniors Outreach Director for the Biden Presidential Campaign. There is a movie about her life in organizing: *Heather Booth: Changing the World*. She is a member of the consulting group Democracy Partners.

KHADIJAH COSTLEY WHITE is an associate professor in the Department of Journalism and Media Studies at Rutgers University in New Brunswick. A former journalist at PBS, Costley White researches media, power, and politics, especially in regard to race and identity. Her book, *Branding Right-Wing Activism: How the News Media Created the Tea Party* (2018), examines the rise of the Tea Party in online, print, broadcast, and cable news. In addition to her scholarly work, Costley White consults on documentary films and has served the MacArthur Foundation as an external adviser in journalism and media. In 2007 the National Association of Black Journalists and the United Nations awarded her a reporting fellowship to Senegal. In 2020, she won a Whiting Public Engagement Fellowship for her community media project on lockdown culture in schools. Costley White's writing and commentary on topics such as race, social movements, news, and politics has appeared in *Vice*, National Public Radio, *The Atlantic*, the *New York Times*, *The Root*, *Huffington Post*, BBC, the *Washington Post*, the *Los Angeles Times*, *Quartz*, *Gizmodo*, *Buzzfeed*, and more. In her local community, Costley White is also an activist, organizer, and a founding executive director of *SOMA Justice*, a community nonprofit that focuses on racial, social, and economic justice.

NANCY FRASER is the Henry A. and Louise Loeb Professor at the New School for Social Research, a visiting research professor at Dartmouth College, and the holder of an international research chair at the Collège d'études mondiales. Trained as a philosopher, she specializes in critical social theory and political philosophy. Her newest book is *Cannibal*

Capitalism: How Our System Is Devouring Democracy, Care and the Planet—and What We Can Do about It (2022). Other recent books include *Feminism for the 99%: A Manifesto*, coauthored with Cinzia Arruzza and Tithi Bhattacharya (2019); *The Old Is Dying* (2019); and *Capitalism: A Conversation in Critical Theory*, coauthored with Rahel Jaeggi (2018). Fraser has theorized capitalism's relation to racial oppression, social reproduction, ecological crisis, feminist movements, and the rise of right-wing populism in a series of linked essays in *New Left Review*, *Critical Historical Studies*, *American Affairs*, and in *Fortunes of Feminism: From State-Managed Capitalism to Neoliberal Crisis* (2013). Her work has been translated into more than twenty languages and was cited twice by the Brazilian Supreme Court (in decisions upholding marriage equality and affirmative action). A Chevalier of the French Legion of Honor, a Member of the American Academy of Arts and Sciences, and a past president of the American Philosophical Association, Eastern Division, she is the recipient of six honorary degrees, the Alfred Schutz Prize for Social Philosophy, and the Nessim Habif World Prize.

SABINE HARK is a professor of interdisciplinary gender studies and the director of the Center for Interdisciplinary Women's and Gender Studies at Technische Universitaet Berlin. Hark is also a prominent public intellectual who regularly intervenes in debates on democracy, racism, sexism, and gender equality. Their books include *deviante Subjekte: Die paradoxe Politik der Identitaet* (Deviant Subjects: Paradoxes of the Politics of Identity) (1996, 1999); *Dissidente Partizipation: Eine Diskursgeschichte des Feminismus* (Dissident Participation: A Discourse History of Feminism) (2005); *Vermessene Raeume, gespannte Beziehungen: Unternehmerische Universitaeten und Geschlechterdynamiken* (Measured Spaces, Tense Relations: Entrepreneurial

Universities and Gender Dynamics), with Johanna Hofbauer (2018), *The Future of Difference: Beyond the Toxic Entanglement of Racism, Sexism and Feminism*, with Paula-Irene Villa (2020), and *Gemeinschaft der Ungewaehlten: Umrisse eines politischen Ethos der Kohabitation* (Community of the Unchosen: Notes on a Political Ethos of Cohabitation) (2021). Hark is a member of the editorial board of Germany's leading feminist theory journal, *Feministische Studien*.

JYL JOSEPHSON is a professor of political science and women's and gender studies at Rutgers University–Newark. She is the author of *Rethinking Sexual Citizenship*. She has written on gender, sexuality, and public policy, primarily in the context of U.S. social policy. Her research has also been published in journals such as *Politics and Gender*, *Journal of Poverty*, *New Political Science*, *Perspectives on Politics*, and *Trans Studies Quarterly*. She has taught community organizing at Rutgers–Newark since 2016. Her course gives political science majors and minors an opportunity to work with community organizations engaged in democratic change and renewal in northern New Jersey. The class, designed in conjunction with organizer Frank McMillan, is an attempt to create an "outside in" university—one where students' research and other activities are designed specifically to meet the needs of the community organization, rather than the university. A resident of Jersey City, she is involved in activism around housing and education issues there.

L. A. KAUFFMAN is a longtime grassroots organizer and movement historian. She is the author of *Direct Action: Protest and the Reinvention of American Radicalism* (2017) and *How to Read a Protest: The Art of Organizing and Resistance* (2018). Kauffman played a leading role in direct-action campaigns that saved more than 100 community gardens and two historic public libraries from destruction in New York City, and she was the mobilizing coordinator for some of the largest demonstrations in U.S. history, the massive Iraq anti-war protests of 2003 and 2004. She is a cofounder of Fair for All, a group that has worked to eliminate Confederate flags from rural county fairs in New York State, and of Remove Trump, which staged daily protests in Washington, D.C., throughout congressional impeachment proceedings in 2019 and 2020. Kauffman has written for *The Guardian*, *Frieze*, *Boston Review*, *The Nation*, and many other publications, and her work has been featured in the *New Yorker*, *Washington Post*, *New York Times*, *New Republic*, and numerous other outlets.

CYNTHIA MILLER-IDRISS is a professor in the School of Public Affairs and in the School of Education at the American University in Washington, D.C., where she directs the Polarization and Extremism Research and Innovation Lab. Miller-Idriss serves on the international advisory board of the Center for Research on Extremism (C-REX) in Oslo, Norway, and is a member of the Southern Poverty Law Center (SPLC)'s Tracking Hate and Extremism Advisory Committee. Her most recent books are *Hate in the Homeland: The New Global Far Right* (2020) and *The Extreme Gone Mainstream: Commercialization and Far Right Youth Culture in Germany* (2018). In addition to her academic work, Miller-Idriss writes frequently for the mainstream press, both as an opinion columnist at MSNBC and in a variety of other national and global media outlets, and also appears regularly in global print and broadcast media as an expert source and political commentator. Dr. Miller-Idriss has testified several times before the U.S. Congress and regularly briefs policy, security, education, and intelligence agencies in the United States, the United Nations, and in other countries on trends in domestic violent extremism and strategies for prevention and disengagement. She holds a PhD and an MA in sociology and a master's in public policy from the University of Michigan, and a BA (magna cum laude) in sociology and German area studies from Cornell University.

VALENTINE M. MOGHADAM is a professor of sociology and international affairs at Northeastern University, Boston. Born in Tehran, Iran, she received her higher education in Canada and the United States. In addition to her academic career, she has been a coordinator of the Research Program on Women and Development at the UNU's WIDER Institute (Helsinki, 1990–1995) and a section chief on gender equality and development, UNESCO's Social and Human Sciences Sector (Paris, 2004–2006). Her areas of research include globalization, transnational social movements and feminist networks, economic citizenship, and gender and development in the Middle East and North Africa. Among her many publications, she is the author of *Modernizing Women: Gender and Social Change in the Middle East* (1993; 2nd ed., 2003; rev. and updated 3rd ed., 2013); *Globalizing Women: Transnational Feminist Networks* (2005), which won the American Political Science Association's Victoria Schuck award for best book on women and politics for 2005; and *Globalization and Social Movements: The Populist Challenge and Democratic Alternatives* (2020). She has edited seven books, including *Empowering Women after the Arab Spring* (2016, with Marwa Shalaby). She coauthored, with Shamiran Mako, *After the Arab Uprisings: Progress and Stagnation in the Middle East and North Africa* (2021). She is a board member of Peace Action, Massachusetts Peace Action, and the Feminist Foreign Policy Project.

SCOT NAKAGAWA is a community organizer, activist, cultural worker, and political writer. He has spent the last four decades exploring questions of racial injustice and racial formation and effective forms of resistance and strategies for change through community campaigns, cultural organizing, popular education, writing, and direct political advocacy. Scot's primary work has been in the fight against vigilante white supremacist groups, white nationalism, Nativism, and authoritarian evangelical political movements. He has served as a strategist, organizer, and social movement analyst for the National Gay and Lesbian Task Force, the Western Prison Project, and the Highlander Center, among others. He is the cofounder and codirector of the 22nd Century Initiative, a national strategy and action hub in the growing movement to defeat authoritarianism and white nationalism. Scot is a past Alston/Bannerman Fellow, Equality Fellow of the Open Society Foundations, and the Association of Asian American Studies 2017 community leader. He is the writer of The Anti-Authoritarian Playbook, a blog providing analysis and strategic advice for pro-democracy activists. His writings have been included in *Race, Gender, and Class in the United States: An Integrated Study* (9th ed.); *Killing Trayvons: An Anthology of American Violence*; and *Eyes Right! Challenging the Right Wing Backlash*.

ARLENE STEIN is the director of the Institute for Research on Women at Rutgers University, where she is also a distinguished professor of sociology. Her research focuses on the intersection of gender, sexuality, culture, and politics. The author or editor of nine books, she received the American Sociological Association's Simon and Gagnon Award for career contributions to the study of sexualities. Her latest book is *Unbound: Transgender Men and the Transformation of Identity* (2019). She is also the author of *The Stranger Next Door* (2001), an ethnography of a Christian conservative campaign against LGBTQ rights, which explores clashing understandings of religion and sexuality in American culture. An updated edition of the book, which received the Ruth Benedict Book Award, will be published in 2022. She is the coauthor of *Going Public: A Guide for Social Scientists*, a guidebook for publicly engaged scholars. Stein has worked as a community organizer in Richmond, California, an activist for reproductive and LGBTQ rights, and a leader of the anti-Trump resistance in Jersey City, New Jersey, where she lives.

SARAH TOBIAS is the associate director of the Institute for Research on Women at Rutgers University, where she also serves as affiliate faculty in the Women's, Gender, and Sexuality Studies Department. Her work bridges academia and public policy. A feminist theorist and LGBT activist, she is the coauthor of *Policy Issues Affecting Lesbian, Gay, Bisexual, and Transgender Families* (2007) and the coeditor of *Trans Studies: The Challenge to Hetero/Homo Normativities* (2016), which was awarded the 2017 Sylvia Rivera Award for the Best Book in Transgender Studies from the City University of New York Center for Lesbian and Gay Studies. With Nicole R. Fleetwood, she edited *The New Status Quo*, a special issue of *Feminist Formations* (2021). She is the founding editor of *Rejoinder*, an online journal published by the Institute for Research on Women at Rutgers. Prior to joining the institute in January 2010, she spent over 8 years working in the nonprofit sector, where she authored and edited numerous policy-related reports and articles. Tobias has also taught at Rutgers-Newark, the City University of New York (Baruch College and Queens College), and Columbia University. She has a PhD in Political Science from Columbia University and an undergraduate degree from Cambridge University, England.

Index

Adityanath, Yogi, 77, 86–88, 96
Advani, L. K., 95
Afghanistan, 40
Algeria, 32
Alternative für Deutschland, 42, 68
alt-right, 6
American Identity movement, 166
Anti Gender Alliance, 64–65
antigenderism, 5, 13, 58–60, 67–68
Anti-Racist Action, 169
anti-Semitism, 6, 39–40, 55, 144
Arab Spring, 12, 21, 50
asceticism, 77, 84–88, 93–94, 96, 98
authoritarianism, 149, 161–163, 168,
    182; antigenderism and, 13, 67;
    capitalism and, 121; elements of,
    56; feminism and, 3, 19, 62, 146;
    gender and, 6, 60, 63; Hobbes
    and, 11; in Nakagawa, 20;
    organizing and, 21; populism and,
    2; protection and, 28

Ball, James, 37
Beauvoir, Simone de, 64
Belafonte, Harry, 136
Benedict XVI, Pope, 57
Berlusconi, Silvio, 73
Bharatiya Janata Party (BJP), 81,
    85–86, 91, 95
BJP. See Bharatiya Janata Party (BJP)

Black Lives Matter, 21, 51
Bland, Bob, 134, 136, 138, 145
Bolsonaro, Jair, 1–2, 57–58, 73, 87
Booth, Heather, 149–151, 156–158,
    162–163, 166–171
brand culture, 36
branding, 45
Branding of Right-Wing Activism,
    The (Costley White), 32–33
Brazil, 1–2, 57–58, 73
Breedlove, Caitlin, 143, 145
Bretton Woods system, 118
Brexit, 1, 122
Britain. See United Kingdom
Brown, Wendy, 61
Butler, Judith, 57–58, 60

Cagan, Leslie, 134
capitalism: anti-elitism and, 31;
    defined, 128n3; democratization
    and, 110; financialization and,
    110–111; hegemonic crisis of,
    121–127; institutional crisis of,
    116–121; political crisis and,
    111–116; state-managed, 110
Capitol insurrection, 7–8
center-right, 160–161
Chakraborty, Mrinalini, 137, 139
Chaney, James, 150
China, 99, 161

Christchurch shooting, 43
Christian Right, 161
Christou, Miranda, 43
Clark, Septima, 142–143
cleanliness, 91–92
climate change, 38–39, 161
Clinton, Hillary, 133
Collins, Patricia Hill, 51
conspiracy theories, 38–40
Constitutional Sheriffs and Peace
    Officers Association, 164
contractarianism, 10–11
Conway, Kellyanne, 36
CORE (Congress of Racial
    Equality), 135
Costley White, Khadijah, 26, 32–38,
    44–46, 50–51
COVID-19 pandemic, 28, 30, 37–39,
    47, 161
crisis, capitalism and, 115–116
critical race theory, 6–7
culture wars, 4

D.C. Action Lab, 140
Defense of Marriage Act (DOMA),
    151
democracy: antigenderism and, 60,
    67; capitalism and, 110, 117; direct,
    89; ineffectiveness of, 1–2;
    post-truth and, 26–51; protection
    of, 19–22; social, 49–50; threats
    to, 158–163
democratization, 110
demographic change, 43
demonization, of minorities, 2
Devji, Faisal, 90–91
Douglass, Frederick, 171
Duterte, Rodrigo, 73, 87

education, 58, 155–156
Eighteenth Brumaire of Louis
    Bonaparte, The (Marx), 30
Ellman-Golan, Sophie, 137

El Paso shooting, 43
Enck-Wanzer, Darrel, 45
Enloe, Cynthia, 76
Erdoğan, Recep Tayyip, 31, 42,
    74, 76
ethnicity, 43. See also race
expertise, 37, 46–47

facts, 36–37
"fake news," 3
Farmer, James, 135
Farrakhan, Louis, 144
Far Right, 28–29, 39–40, 43
Fekete, Liz, 68
femininity, 42, 44, 59, 76, 98
feminism, 5, 9, 12, 45; future
    through lens of, 46–51; intersec-
    tional, 145–146; in Middle East
    and North Africa, 31–32;
    Women's Marches and, 131–132
femonationalism, 42
Fields, Barbara Jean, 170
financialization, 110–112, 116–121,
    128n3
Foucault, Michel, 61
France, 9, 58, 66
Frances, Pope, 57
Freedom Summer, 150
fundamentalism, 41–42, 68

Gandhi, M. K., 76–77, 82, 85, 88–89,
    91–95
Gandhi, Rahul, 83–84
gender, 3–7, 41–44, 46; and
    antigenderism, 58–59; authoritari-
    anism and, 6, 60, 63; Catholic
    Church on, 57; in Goffman,
    63–64; in Kuby, 56; neoliberalism
    and, 51; in Pope Frances, 57;
    post-truth and, 38; social
    engineering and, 59–60
Gender and the Politics of History
    (Scott), 64

gender ideology, 5, 57–59, 61, 63, 64, 66
genderism, 61
gender studies, 62
Germany, 42, 56, 58–59, 64–65
globalization, 17, 31, 60–61, 78, 89, 93, 181
Globalization and Social Movements (Moghadam), 31
global populism, 30–32
Global Sexual Revolution, The: Destruction of Freedom in the Name of Freedom (Kuby), 56
Global South, 27–28
Godse, Nathuram, 85
Goffman, Erving, 63–64
gold standard, 118
Golwalkar, M. S., 85
Goodman, Andrew, 150
"Great Replacement," 43

Hall, Stuart, 60
hegemony, crisis of, 115, 121–127
Hegemony and Socialist Strategy (Laclau and Mouffe), 109–113, 115, 127
Highlander Center, 21
Hobbes, Thomas, 10
homophobia, 18, 72, 74, 144, 146
horizontality, 8
Hungary, 41–42, 58
hypermasculinity, 74, 80

immigration, 29, 43–44, 68, 125, 157–158
inclusion, 8, 61, 143
India, 72–73, 75, 80–99
Industrial Areas Foundation, 21
institutional crisis, 115–121
intersectionality, 15, 47, 139, 144–146
Iraq War, 32, 41
Islam, 31–32, 42, 44
Italy, 73

January 6 insurrection, 7–8
Jordan, 31
Josephson, Jyl, 149, 151, 155–156, 158–160, 170–171

Katsav, Moshe, 73
Kavanaugh, Brett, 139
Keskinen, Suvi, 42
Keynesianism, 119
Khan, Omaima, 145
King, Martin Luther, Jr., 135–136, 142
Klein, Hans-Peter, 62
Kuby, Gabriele, 56, 59, 61, 66
Ku Klux Klan, 150

Laclau, Ernesto, 109–111, 122, 125, 127
leadership, 77–84
left-wing populism, 7–9, 122
Lenin, Vladimir, 30
Le Pen, Marine, 9, 66, 68
Leviathan (Hobbes), 10
LGBTQ rights, 4, 151–152, 155
Libya, 32
Lumumba, Patrice, 40

Mahabharata, 96–97
Mallory, Tamika, 136, 144–145
"Mama Grizzlies," 35
Manne, Kate, 133
March for Women's Lives, 134
March on Washington for Jobs and Freedom, 134
Marx, Karl, 30
Marxism, 49, 109, 111–112, 114, 127
masculinity, 11, 43, 59, 74, 80, 98
Mayer, Tamar, 79–80
McRobbie, Angela, 45
media, 3, 17, 32–37, 77, 137–138
#MeToo, 51
Middle East, 31–32, 49–50
Midwest Academy, 20

Miller-Idriss, Cynthia, 26–28, 38–40, 43–44, 46–48
Mir, Noor, 140
misinformation, 37, 39–40, 46–47
Modi, Narendra, 72–73, 75–77, 80–84, 86–98
Moffitt, Benjamin, 77
Moghadam, Valentine M., 26, 30–31, 40–42, 49–50
Morocco, 31–32
Mouffe, Chantal, 109–111, 122, 125, 127
Mudde, Cas, 2
Müller, Ursula, 63
multiculturalism, 27, 43, 124
Muslim Brotherhood, 31

Nakagawa, Scot, 20, 149, 152–155, 160–166, 170–171
Nandy, Ashis, 84
National Democratic Alliance (India), 81
nationalism, 9, 12, 27–30, 42, 78–79, 124, 164–165
Nation of Islam, 144
nativism, 30–31, 182
neoliberalism, 2, 5–6, 21, 31, 110, 112, 120, 123–124, 126–127, 128n3
New Left, 109
North Africa, 31–32, 49–50

Oath Keepers, 20, 164, 170
Obama, Barack, 44

Palin, Sarah, 35
pandemic. See COVID-19 pandemic
Pantsuit Nation (Facebook group), 133
Parks, Rosa, 133
Perez, Carmen, 136, 145
Perry, Alonzo, 159–160
Philippines, 73
pluralism, 8, 77

polarization, 9, 40, 46–48, 55
populism: defining, 27–30, 78; global, 30–32; left-wing, 7–9, 122; media and, 32–35; progressive, 14, 125–126; reactionary, 14, 125–127
Populist Party, 34
Posse Comitatus, 164
postfeminist, 38, 44, 46
postracial, 38, 44–46
post-truth: Black feminism and, 12; brand culture and, 36; defined, 3, 36; democracy and, 26–51; social media and, 21; subjectivity and, 45
progressive neoliberalism, 110, 123, 126–127
progressive populism, 14, 125–126
purity, 91–92
Putin, Vladimir, 73–74, 76

race: in critical race theory, 6–7; mobilization around, 43, 45; neoliberalism and, 51; post-truth and, 38; Tea Party and, 33, 35
Rashtriya Sawayamsevak Sangh (RSS), 75, 85–86, 92
Ratzinger, Joseph, 57
reactionary neoliberalism, 123–124
reactionary populism, 14, 125–127
relational organizing, 158–159
religious fundamentalism, 41–42, 68
renunciation, 72, 76, 86, 96–97
Republican Party, 20, 33, 160, 165
respectability, 91–92
right-wing populism, 4–7, 9–10, 19–20, 26, 30. See also Far Right
RSS. See Rashtriya Sawayamsevak Sangh (RSS)
Rural Organizing Project (ROP), 168
Russia, 30, 73–74

Sanders, Bernie, 8
Santelli, Rick, 33–34

Sarsour, Linda, 136, 145
schools, 58, 155–156
Schwarner, Michael, 150
Schwarzer, Alice, 59
Scott, Joan W., 64
Seraw, Mulugeta, 160
sexual assault, 133
Shah, Amit, 89
Skinheads Against Racial
    Prejudice, 169
Skolnik, Michael, 136
social contract theory, 10–11
social engineering, 59–60
social media, 3, 21, 37–39, 50–51, 133
Soros, George, 40
Stern, Alexandra Minna, 6
subjectivity, 45, 51
success, models of, 48
Syria, 32

Tea Party, 32–35, 38, 45
textbooks, 58
Three Percenters, 20, 164
Trump, Donald: alt-right and,
    6; antigovernment and, 29;
    Christian Right and, 161;
    COVID-19 pandemic and, 37;
    judicial appointments of, 163–164;
    masculinity and, 87; mobilization
    against, 131–133; Modi versus, 87,
    99; populist performance of, 76;
    post-truth and, 2–3, 37; Putin on,
    73–74; radical Right and, 20; in
    rise of populism, 1, 122; Women's
    Marches and, 131–146; women
    who voted for, 42
Tunisia, 31–32, 50
Turkey, 31, 42, 74
Turning Point USA, 166

United Kingdom, 1, 122

vaccine denialism, 37
Vietnam War, 40

Wacquant, Loïc, 2
Washington Consensus, 118
Westerling, Marcy, 168
white nationalism, 6, 20, 160,
    164–166, 170, 182
white supremacy, 6, 29–30, 47
women, 4, 11, 42, 78–79, 87
Women's Liberation Movement, 139
Women's Marches, 131–146

Printed in the United States
by Baker & Taylor Publisher Services